011

£3.50

D0548286

£

0 031140 032361

HOMETOWN TALES
WALES

HOMETOWN TALES is a series of books pairing exciting new voices with some of the most talented and important authors at work today. Each of the writers has contributed an original tale on the theme of hometown, exploring places and communities in the UK where they have lived or think of as home.

Some of the tales are fiction and some are narrative non-fiction – they are all powerful, fascinating and moving, and aim to celebrate regional diversity and explore the meaning of home.

HOMETOWN TALES
WALES

TYLER KEEVIL
ELUNED GRAMICH

W&N
WEIDENFELD & NICOLSON

First published in Great Britain in 2018 by Weidenfeld & Nicolson
an imprint of The Orion Publishing Group Ltd
Carmelite House, 50 Victoria Embankment
London EC4Y 0DZ

An Hachette UK Company

1 3 5 7 9 10 8 6 4 2

Last Seen Leaving © Tyler Keevil 2018
The Lion and the Star © Eluned Gramich 2018

The moral right of Tyler Keevil and Eluned Gramich to be identified
as the authors of this work has been asserted in accordance
with the Copyright, Designs and Patents Act of 1988.

All rights reserved. No part of this publication may be reproduced, stored in
a retrieval system, or transmitted in any form or by any means, electronic,
mechanical, photocopying, recording, or otherwise, without the prior
permission of both the copyright owner and the above publisher of this book.

Although set in real places, the tales and characters in this book
are fictitious, and any resemblance to actual persons, living or dead,
is purely coincidental.

Certain names and identifying characteristics have, on occasion,
been changed to protect the privacy of individuals.

A CIP catalogue record for this book is available from the British Library.

ISBN (Hardback) 978 1 4746 0871 8
ISBN (eBook) 978 1 4746 0872 5

Typeset at The Spartan Press Ltd,
Lymington, Hants

Printed and bound in Great Britain by Clays Ltd, Elcograf S.p.A.

www.orionbooks.co.uk

CONTENTS

Last Seen Leaving

Tyler Keevil

TYLER KEEVIL grew up in Vancouver and in his mid-twenties moved to Wales. He is the author of several books and his short fiction has appeared in a wide range of magazines and anthologies, including *The Missouri Review*, *New Welsh Review*, and *PRISM: International*. He has received a number of awards for his work, most notably *The Missouri Review*'s Jeffrey E. Smith Editors' Prize, The Writers' Trust of Canada / McClelland & Stewart Journey Prize, and the Wales Book of the Year People's Prize. He is a Lecturer in Creative Writing at Cardiff University, and his latest novel, *No Good Brother*, is published by The Borough Press.

ALAN WENT MISSING on a Wednesday. Or maybe it was a Thursday. I can't actually remember, but I know the exact date: November 3rd. So it was definitely around this same time of year, near Halloween and Guy Fawkes. Maybe that's why I've been thinking about him lately: the climate calls to mind that time and period in our lives. The frost-stiff grass; the bone-bare branches; the reddish leaves scuttling along the gutters like crabs; the occasional, ominous detonation of fireworks disrupting the homely quiet; the foggy stench of sulphur and mulch, of endings and decay: all these details bring back memories of our life in Mid Wales, and that period in particular.

I know the exact date because it was prominent on the posters Deborah, Alan's wife, put around town shortly after his disappearance. She printed them on

3

her computer and taped them to lamp posts and notice-boards and in shop windows. She asked me to put a few up, too, and I did – though I kept one. I do this: collect mementos, keepsakes, curios, evidence. I have drawers and filing cabinets full of strange items and objects, such as broken watch straps and carved figurines and penknives and crumpled letters from people back home in Canada. I even have keys to some of the flats and houses where Mari and I have lived. Mari thinks I'm crazy; she isn't prone to such romantic attachments and can't fathom why I keep all these things together, secreted away. It's as if, through the objects, I'm trying to create a nest of sense. And at times I peer into the drawers and see a kind of pattern, a rhyme and reason, a logical progression. Other times, I discover nothing but clutter, chaos, a meaningless menagerie. Some of the bits and pieces I can no longer remember why I kept, or even where they came from.

Alan's missing poster is in one of the drawers, along with the name tag he had made for us workers at his company, Custom Circuit Design, or CCD. I worked for him for several years: first in the garage behind his house and then, later, at the industrial unit he rented when he made the decision to expand. Alan designed, and we made, printed circuit boards for various devices, such as water pumps, air conditioners, fans heaters, and the like. It was a niche market and he did fairly well at it, for a time

The poster header describes Alan as 'missing', though in the photo he of course doesn't look lost or absent or 'missing' in any way. He is smiling and holding up a pint of lager, probably Carlsberg, which is what he always drank. A middle-aged man with thinning blonde hair and a lean, longish face. I have studied the photo. Its selection for the poster was probably partly due to chance: just a picture Deborah had on hand and thought a good likeness, chosen at a time when she must have been under unimaginable stress. But to me it also feels somehow appropriate to the whole mystery. His expression seems inconsistent, by turns anxious, merry, surly, smug, morose, mischievous: enigmatic as a Guy Fawkes mask. Or a hologram that shifts this way and that, depending on the angle, type and quality of light, refraction, the viewer's mood. In seeking answers in the photo, I come up, again and again, against the unknowable, the unfathomable.

The caption lists his height (6'1") and weight (190lbs) and age (46), and describes him as last seen leaving the White Lion pub, on the night of

November 3rd, wearing jeans and a blue fleece. I know that fleece, and have one myself. When things were going well, Alan ordered them for us, along with hats and T-shirts emblazoned with the company logo: a lightning bolt zig-zagging through the letters 'CCD'. Uniforms, he called them, though it was the novelty that appealed. Alan appreciated that aspect of running his own business: the camaraderie, the team spirit, the sense of belonging and cohesion. We had pub nights and staff meals and BBQs at his house. The uniforms were part of that. He didn't really expect us to wear them. Or, he never said as much.

He was like that, though, in the way he conducted himself. A lot was left unsaid, unspoken. I know that now more than I did at the time.

*

On the day the posters went up, Branwen – one of our old colleagues from CCD – texted me, asking whether I'd seen the noticeboard outside Spar. Her message ended in multiple exclamation marks. I hadn't seen the board, and in looking back, it is hard to know whether I sensed, then, that it was to do with Alan. I don't think that I did. But before replying to Branwen, I went down to the local Spar to find out what she meant.

I say 'local' but in reality everything in our town was local. The layout, and composition, comes back easily. Sometimes I dream we still live there, or wake forgetting that we have moved. In dreams and reality the town is the same: arranged in a cross with a clock tower in the centre, constructed centuries before the advent of automobiles, when roads were narrower. As a result, the clock causes great tangles of traffic whenever a tractor or farm vehicle or lorry (what I would call a sixteen-wheeler) has to manoeuvre around it. As is common in small towns, or at least small Welsh towns, the majority of businesses cluster together there, at the crossroads, as if seeking some solidarity against the superstores and shopping centres – those great motherships of commerce – that often seem to land overnight, descending on the unsuspecting populace, who are drawn to the lights, the warmth, the glossy signs, and quickly learn to accept their dominance, unwitting as livestock.

Our town – at that time – had managed to avoid being targeted. It wasn't quite big enough to warrant such attention or expansions. It meant that many of the small businesses managed to eke out a living, due to the loyalty of locals and the needs of tourists. The high street contained an antique furniture store, an electrical goods shop with a Euronics logo in the window, a second-hand bookshop, a butcher and baker, various charity shops (cancer, cats, care homes), and numerous pubs, including the Lion, where Alan was last seen. At the end of the main strip sits the Spar. Some of the other businesses have closed, or changed hands, since we left, but the few times we've passed back through – largely for the sake of nostalgia – I've always been surprised not by the noticeable changes, but the seeming quality of sameness and consistency in the townscape. This is particularly in contrast to Vancouver, and Canadian cities, which grow and spread and self-consume like monsters, oblivious to the past or planning permission. No, the town – our town – seems the opposite of that: as enduring and steadfast as the hitching stone that still sits in front of the Rider's Inn. Only now, instead of horses, people use it to lock up their bikes.

Our house was on the same side of town as the Spar – just a short walk away, past the empty lot and MOT garage. An access ramp led up to the front doors, and a noticeboard was hung in the window, facing out, where people could display vehicles for sale, job vacancies and other bits of local news. I spotted the poster immediately, and stood huddled outside staring at it, shocked, my fingers cold and stiffening from the November chill. Something about the act seemed apt for the setting, like an old photo of villagers standing outside their town shop, reading the latest news or notices from London, or New York, or the front line.

Only, in this case, it was the home front, a very local story. I peered at Alan's face – obscured slightly by grease on the glass. Under the heading, there was a subheading: *Have you seen this man?* At first glance, you could have mistaken it for a wanted poster – the kind used to catch a criminal. Except the contact number wasn't the local constabulary, but Deborah's mobile. I stared at it until my face and hands had gone numb (in my hurry I hadn't thought to grab my jacket). Eventually, I slipped my phone from my pocket and snapped a photo of the poster, to show Mari, before trudging home, my head bowed, my shoulders hunched against the cold and the chill. I felt, and must have looked, anxious, furtive, bashful. And guilty.

*

The night of Alan's disappearance, several of us had been with him in the pub, including Branwen and myself, and Deborah too – in the early part of the evening. We had arranged to go out for a 'works do', or what I would call a staff party. We still did things like that, even though we were no longer working together. CCD had folded during the recession – and by that I mean the most recent recession, in what seems to have become an endless series of recessions, one leading into the next. A slow bleed of commerce, and of livelihoods. One by one, Alan had been forced to let us go. Since I was the first one he had hired, I was the last to be made redundant, and he had filed for bankruptcy shortly after. He called me up to tell me, with a cheerful defiance. It was a domino effect, he said. He had ordered supplies for jobs and together we'd completed them, sinking money and hours into the task, but ultimately the buyers couldn't pay, which meant he was stuck with useless circuit boards and huge overhead costs, which the banks had eventually called in. When I asked him what he would do now, he said, 'Fuck knows. Look after the kids, I guess.' Then, after a few seconds, he added, 'Thank Christ the house is in Deborah's name.' I don't actually know if losing his house was a real danger (from what I've heard, business debts rarely cross over with personal debts), but I suppose it was possible, and it made for a dramatic statement. Either way, the fate of CCD seemed inevitable – so many businesses were closing then – and I appreciated the stoic way Alan had faced this misfortune, maintaining a stiff upper lip. A very British phrase, though we have our equivalents: take it on the chin, suck it up, man up. These terms that were drilled into me growing up, and which I cling to in times of loss and failure. Small mantras that are by turns life-saving and debilitating.

I, of course, knew Alan was doing that, putting on a brave face, but I didn't consider until later just how much the closure of CCD might have stung him: the disintegration of the team he had built, and for which he had such fondness and affection. That was why we still went out for meals, drinks, get-togethers: it was a way of maintaining that team spirit, even though with each meeting we felt more like strangers, had drifted further into our separate lives, with new jobs, new colleagues.

On the night he disappeared we went out for a curry at the White Lion. That tradition seems so natural now that I've lived in Britain for so many years, but before moving from Vancouver the concept would have been completely alien to me. You go to a restaurant for a curry. You go to a pub to drink.

That said, we don't really have pubs back home – we have bars – so the differences don't stop there.

The Lion is halfway down the high street and has a large statue of a lion above the door, notable for its enormous testicles, which are larger than life and slightly tarnished from drunks jumping up to slap or grab them – in the same way parts of certain religious statues have a different sheen from pilgrims and penitents who touch, say, Christ's feet, or Mary's upturned hand. Inside, the pub has a low ceiling on the verge of collapse, the ancient beams bowed impossibly under the weight of the rooms above. In one corner sits a huge cast-iron stove, decorated with brass pans and pots, the whole contraption looking like a scaled-down version of a science fiction loco-motive, a steampunk set piece.

We sat around a low table on faded red leather sofas and leaned forward to eat our plates of korma and bhuna and madras. The meal now looms large in my memory, since it was the night of what happened, but in truth it was significant before that: it was the evening Mari and I shared the news that we were expecting. Though I don't think we used those words. I probably just said, 'We're going to have a baby,' or 'Mari's pregnant.' I do remember that, after the collective expression of delight and congratulations dwindled, Alan tipped back his head and guffawed, opening his mouth wide, showing teeth and tongue, as if trying to catch a piece of food he'd tossed up. He said to me, 'You? A father? Just wait. Just wait!' He said it jokingly, but perhaps with a bit more edge than he'd intended (by that point we were a few beers deep). I don't think it was just me that noted it. Deborah put her hand on his forearm and smiled supportively at me and said, 'He'll be a great dad.' Alan nodded vigorously, perhaps sensing that he had overstepped. 'I didn't mean *that*,' he said, without then going on to explain what he had meant.

After the meal we ordered another round, but by that point Deborah had begun to doze. Not because she was drunk (she'd only had two halves) but because she was so weary. She tilted her head sideways and rested it on Alan's shoulder and closed her eyes. Noticing, Alan said, 'That's what parenthood will do to you.' As he called a cab for her, Mari and I exchanged a look, both anxious and thrilled that those challenges would be ours soon enough.

Later, after Deborah had left – and Mari too, since she wasn't drinking – Alan and I stood at the bar and

13

ordered whiskies. The other people in our team –
Branwen, Mike, Ellen – were our age but their kids
were much older, since they'd had them in their early
twenties. Mike was necking cider and Branwen and
Ellen were sharing a bottle of house white, singing
along to the jukebox. Alan and I leaned at the bar,
mimicking each other with our poses, and held up
the whiskies. He'd wanted to buy me one by way of
celebration, and asked me to pick any of the top-shelf
bottles. I'd ordered Talisker and the bartender – who
knew us both – repeated the name in my accent,
twanging the last syllable in a way that sounded
American to me, not Canadian at all. But to him the
difference wasn't so much. One of those constant,
everyday reminders of my foreignness and otherness.

We sipped our Talisker like gentlemen, and if we'd
had cigars – if smoking was still allowed in pubs – no
doubt we would have been puffing on them, too. Our
wives had gone home and though we were talking
to each other, occasionally our eyes would wander
over to the singing women who kept beckoning us
to come back, to join them. It was the unspoken rule
that things got louder, more raucous, more fun, when
Mari and Deborah had left.

By that point I'd had half a dozen pints and the

night was beginning to slide away, in the way it does. But I remember Alan swirling his whisky and looking into it, as if reading tea leaves, and telling me that marriage, for them, hadn't changed anything. 'But kids,' he said, 'That changes everything.' I said something diplomatic, along the lines of it all being worth it in the end. And he was quick to agree – again as if compensating for being too forthright. He knocked back his Talisker and Branwen called to us from across the room: they wanted to do a quiz on the machine, and though I was hopeless, Alan knew music. He was good at questions about British pop from previous decades: groups like The Troggs and Yes and Wet Wet Wet.

We ordered two more whiskies – cheaper doubles, this time – and carried them across the room. Branwen drew us into the group, looping an arm around Alan. She smelled sweaty and perfume-sweet, a scent I knew very well from having sat so often with her in the workshop. She raised her glass to CCD, and we all drank. At one time it would have been earnest and fervent, such a toast. Now it had to be sad, ironic, a little bit of a joke. And a good excuse to have another drink.

*

The weight of that evening hung heavy on me as I trudged back up the street to our house. A mist had settled on the surrounding hills overnight, and the air had the damp, clammy quality that leaches into your bones. It seemed appropriate for the time of year. The mists created a kind of chiaroscuro effect, that softening of detail with distance you see in landscape painting. It gave the town a feeling of being cocooned and cut off from outside happenings.

Our place was on a terrace near the bypass: part of a double row of opposing homes divided by an alley that only allowed for pedestrian access. We had bought it in our early twenties – far younger than any of my friends were buying back home, an act that to them seemed almost scandalously mature and practical. But we did so mostly because we'd been previously renting a flat riddled with damp and mould that had begun to play hell with Mari's lungs; she'd had asthma as a kid and the mould brought it out again. The landlord refused to do anything about it and we realised that property was so cheap in Mid Wales (flats and terraces went for under fifty thousand pounds) and mortgage rates so good, we could buy a small terraced house with very little down and pay a monthly mortgage fee far less than we were paying in rent. After we moved, the flat was condemned and the landlord was never able to rent it out again, a triumph that I still recall with grim satisfaction.

The new place was small – what the British call a 'two-up two-down', with a narrow strip of garden out the back – but it was warm and cosy rather than damp and mouldy. And it was ours. We had devoutly begun a series of do-it-yourself repairs, an impulse that Mari's mother had fondly dubbed 'nesting' in the hopes that it was a step towards us starting a family of our own, which in fact it had turned out to be. In our nesting we were guided only by a copy of the Collins DIY book, big as a bible, which had been gifted to us by Alan: an old version that he and Deborah had used when they'd first bought their place outside of town. The difference lay in the fact that Alan was very handy – being a qualified electrician and engineer – whereas Mari and I were both happily inept, despite the basics skills I'd picked up working at CCD. Still, we tried. We stripped floorboards, knocked down partition walls, slapped up wallpaper, painted the bathroom upstairs. We even measured, ordered, and installed a fitted kitchen bought from one of the big British chains: an achievement that still seems miraculous to me, given our level of ability.

Alan helped, actually. He'd warned me against trying any of the electrics myself, since the wiring was dodgy in those older houses (as he put it). Out of pride and misplaced confidence, I'd tried, but after nearly electrocuting myself installing the oven, I sheepishly called him up and he came over to help me with the wiring for the oven, and also the lights and cooker hood. I bought a case of Carlsberg and we worked and drank and he explained what he was doing in the same patient way he did at the industrial unit. With his help, we finished that particular job, and went on to others. The place was run-down, but solid, enduring. The whole terrace had once housed factory workers for a local foundry, long-since defunct, a coincidence I appreciated since I'd also become a factory worker, of sorts. At least for a time. At least until our factory went the same way as the foundry.

Our front door opened directly into that kitchen. I stepped inside and shut the door behind me and stood rubbing my elbows and shifting from foot to foot, in a pantomime performance of warming up. Mari stood at the stove in her fluffy white bathrobe and slippers, brewing coffee in a stovetop cafetière that, if mis-assembled or not attended to, had the tendency to explode in a scalding bomb of coffee grounds. The heating was on and it was pleasantly warm and I could smell the roast grounds and she glanced back at me and smiled politely. The day before, we had argued about my staying out so late, and getting so drunk – again – and in my hung-over state I'd said some defensive, unpleasant things. That argument was still percolating, like the coffee, and in truth it had been brewing on and off for the four months since Mari had gotten pregnant. Even so, those tensions seemed everyday, and very normal, compared to the news I was about to share.

I did not know how to broach it – and didn't want to do so when her back was turned – so I sat at the table and ceremoniously laid my phone out atop it, with the screen visible. I clasped my hands solemnly and bowed my head, as if in prayer. As my hands warmed up they began to tingle and sting, charged by the painful return of blood and life. I waited until Mari had placed a mug of steaming coffee down in front of us both. Then I nudged the phone, with subtle drama, and said, 'Alan's missing.'

She looked at me curiously – either baffled by my blunt statement, or the odd way I had chosen to pass this on – and then sat and peered at the phone with the same intensity you might study a map, using her fingers to enlarge the image. I reached for my coffee, cupping the mug without drinking it, feeling the burn through the skin of my palms. I had that sense of alteration that descends when our routine is disrupted. It's often described as surreal, or unreal, but in my experience the opposite is true: it feels *more* real, hyperreal, as if the everyday reality is illusion, whereas crisis, danger, accident, tragedy, frailty, is the truth that lurks behind it, a truth we have to ignore simply in order to function. Only, every so often something happens, something like this, and the truth demands our attention.

Was I feeling these things at the time? Possibly not. But it seems to me the memory I have in my head of Mari's expression as she studied my photo of the poster reflects something of that. She had been expecting to sit with me and enjoy our morning coffee, perhaps discuss plans for turning my study into the nursery, and now this disturbance, this strangeness. Without being aware of it, she had instinctively put her hand to her belly, as if seeking to shield our unborn child from whatever was going on.

When she'd absorbed it, we looked at each other in disbelief, and reached for the kind of stock phrases that people do in times of stress, and duress. I mean things like: 'I can't believe it' and 'This is so terrible' and 'It must be a mistake' – exchanges that aren't particularly interesting and in no way contribute to the arc of this story, or the real story that lurks behind it. It was only after we had released the steam of our incredulity that we adopted a more practical tact. Mari asked, 'Do you think he left her?'

I held out my hands in a helpless gesture, as if to imply 'Who knows?' Then I shook my head. 'I can't see that,' I said. 'Nothing I ever saw or heard made me think that might be going on in his head.'

I had finished my coffee – gulping it in swift mouthfuls – and now I got up to pour some more. I could feel the hornet buzz of caffeine, making me jittery, and didn't like the thought – or the possibility – that Alan had just left like that. Done a runner. Wasn't that what they called it?

'Look,' I said, 'there are only a few possibilities.'

Then I stopped, not going on to list them. I had heard my own voice and it sounded absurd. In addition, I hadn't really considered the full gamut of possibilities. But Mari was looking at me, waiting patiently, so I had to go on. I did so, emphasising each possibility by chopping ridiculously with my free hand, like a politician laying out policies.

'Maybe he did take off. Maybe he left – he just had to do it overnight, instantly, since if he'd tried to talk it out, been around her and the kids, he wouldn't have been able to do it. In which case he'll still have to get in touch soon.'

Saying it like that made it sound more possible. Probable, even.

'Or he got too drunk,' I added, 'and ended up sleeping it off somewhere.'

'That was the night before last.'

I tipped my head back and forth. 'Well, we were hitting it pretty hard until late, or early. I didn't get home until what, two?' I hesitated: we both knew it had been later. 'If they'd kept on it, or Alan had, he could be just coming round – and Deborah over-reacted.'

That option didn't sound convincing, even to me.

'Or else,' I said, 'he's done something, and had to get away.'

'What could he have done?'

I had to think about that. My first thought was money. What with the company, and the bankruptcy, maybe he was being hounded by creditors, or had done something dodgy with the books: he wasn't particularly meticulous about records or finances, which would have been fine, until he had to fold.

'Hell,' I said. 'I don't know.'

Mari put her coffee mug aside. She stood up carefully, moving with the heavy grace of pregnant women, in this case acting as if she was already further along than she was.

'And Deborah made these posters?'

'She must have. It's her number.'

'It just seems odd that she didn't call us,' she said.

'She did.'

It sounded like a confession, and she looked at me, accusingly.

'Yesterday morning. You were at antenatal. I was sleeping.'

'You were passed out.'

I closed my eyes, tried to think back. I still felt hung-over. A two-day hangover. Deborah had rung just before noon, asking after Alan. I'd reassured her, told her what I'd essentially told Mari: that it had been a late one, a final hurrah for CCD. That he was probably just sleeping it off somewhere. Gave no hint that there could be anything more to it.

'I should talk to her,' I said to Mari. 'I should go see her.'

I got out my phone, and it was still open to the thread with Branwen. I began texting back, to say that I'd seen the poster now, that I was going to visit Deborah and check up on her. I had my phone at waist-height, between us, and Mari observed this curiously.

'You're texting Branwen?' she said, her tone deliberately casual.

I paused, looked up. 'She saw the posters first. That's how I knew.'

'I didn't know you and her were like that.'

'This is a particular situation,' I said. 'This is about Alan.'

As if to prove it, I texted him next, asking him where he'd got to, if everything was all right. *We're worried about you.* It was hard to write anything that didn't sound trite, but I still felt obliged to try.

*

To get to Alan and Deborah's place you drove north out of town, past the old lead mines – the buildings mouldering and half-sunk in the autumn muck, like a ship going down – and up a sharp incline with cliffs on the left, occasionally threaded with the ropes of rock climbers, tiny as spiders. To the right, a steep slope of grass and gorse and heather dropped down to the shores of the local reservoir, though, of course, most of the water was not used locally; like so many Welsh reservoirs, it supplied towns and cities in England.

At the top of the hill was a hairpin turn, marked now by a white cross, slightly askew, surrounded by bouquets of flowers, some half-dead and withered, dripping petals, others still fresh, having been placed more recently. The previous summer, a family had gone off the road there. Or they had been forced off. Another driver, going the opposite way, had been overtaking. The family – in their van – had rolled down that slope into the reservoir. They had all drowned except the father, who had repeatedly dived under, trying to save his wife and two children. He had still been trying when the rescue crews arrived, and by then it was too late. It had been national news at the time. All the papers had noted his heroic efforts. The driver – the other driver – was at fault, of course. But still. The articles gave the underlying impression that the father, though clearly blameless, was also to blame. Simply for having survived. For not having tried harder to save them (though he had done all he could). Perhaps for not having died in the process.

I don't know who was driving the family van; that was never mentioned.

It had all occurred around the time my own father was visiting us, from Canada. He and my mother flew out once a year, but occasionally – due to work – at different intervals. He and I had driven by the same spot, and that cross, since it happened to be near the tourist information centre overlooking the reservoir. We had stopped at the café to buy coffee and had wandered along the hilltop, to stretch our legs and take in the view. I'd forgotten about the cross until we came upon it, and then I couldn't really avoid telling him the story.

My father, he's an optimist. He doesn't like to focus too much on the news, and all the accidents and deaths and crimes it delineates. But he's not naïve. In his youth his baby sister died of scarlet fever and when I was a teenager his friend and colleague, the partner in his accountancy firm, had died of cancer. So he has lived through small, everyday tragedies – like anybody that age, I suppose. He simply prefers, in his later years, to avoid dwelling too much on them. But of course it can't always be avoided, and when I unintentionally blindsided him with the story of the drowned family, I recall him peering down that slope, sipping his coffee, squinting at the pristine surface of the reservoir. Imagining. Then he waved a hand, as if swatting away a cloud of flies. 'The poor bastard,' he said, which struck me as odd, but of course sympathy for the dead is lost; they are beyond it. He was thinking of, and identifying with, the father. 'No coming back from that,' he said, definitively, and I knew he had been envisioning a parallel situation: the loss of his wife, my mother, and me, my siblings. Gone. To think the unthinkable. So little residing between happiness and horror. Just a turn of the wheel. An error in judgement, a lapse in concentration. And maybe not even yours: maybe somebody else's. Unforeseen disaster.

It seems almost indulgent to dwell on such thoughts. What's the point? Like my father, the temptation is to wave it away, move on. It hadn't happened. Not to me, anyway. And I still had a hard time, then, imagining those possibilities. It is something about youth, that sense of imperviousness and invulnerability. I truly could not fathom such disaster.

Except. I was getting older. We had been trying, as they say. And Mari and I had gotten a glimmer of such calamities, with her first pregnancy. The little bean, as she'd called it, which made me think of the

BFG, who referred to people as 'human beans'. All of us so helpless and vulnerable. And our bean, our first bean, had shrivelled and died. Too soon to have told anybody, so we were spared the painful social condolences. But we had met it, in the early scans. Mari had held it inside her. And, of course, such thoughts haunted us, as we – she – got further along in this pregnancy. Each day a small achievement. And now other people knew, so it seemed real. But still. We understood it was a gift, not a given.

I turned away from the reservoir, the cross, the information centre, all those thoughts. Heading inland. Alan and Deborah's house was in that direction, about five miles along and partway to the next town. As I drove, I opened a half-empty bottle of Lucozade, left in the car from days ago, and drank it all, warm and flat and sweet as syrup. I had to be sharper, better. Not just for Deborah, but for Mari, too. I had made a mistake – I had made many mistakes – and I needed to believe in this case there was still the chance to set things right, to find Alan.

When Deborah had called the previous morning, I'd fumbled for the phone, answered, terrified that it would be Mari, who'd gone to our antenatal group (where I should have been, too). I lived in simmering fear of unexpected calls, especially from her, because of what had happened with her first pregnancy. That was partly why I'd been drinking so much. Or so I told myself – though such a claim was highly dubious, and admitting it would have ignited an argument with Mari. Either way, I'd been relieved to hear Deborah's voice on the phone, and merely confused when she asked after Alan.

'Oh,' I said, hiding my guardedness behind the veil of my hangover. 'He hasn't come home, yet?'

She confirmed that he hadn't, said that it wasn't like him. I apologised, as if it was my fault – and maybe it was – and went on to assure her that it had been a very late night, that I myself hadn't gotten in until nearly four in the morning, vaguely extending the time, to make his own tardiness seem more probable, and forgivable.

'Was everybody out late?' she asked.

'Most of them were still there, when I left,' I said.

Again it was a partial truth. A half-truth. Lies dredged up from the foggy malaise of sleep and booze. I didn't know how much to say. I didn't know how much I might give away, or even if there was anything to give away. It was a position I hadn't been in for a long time, and my responses were rusty: it reminded me of high school, and university, the madness of those years, the drunken couplings, the frequent infidelities and betrayals. Had he taken it that far? Had he gone home with somebody else?

'I'm sorry, Deborah,' I said, 'I'm pretty hung-over still. I can have a think, if you like, and maybe call around?'

She said she'd really appreciate that. Only I hadn't. I'd gone back to sleep.

The turning came up and I steered onto the track that led to their place: a detached cottage from the fifties, covered in greying stucco, with a triangular-shaped yard extending out the back, overlooking a farmer's field. The yard was surrounded by split-rail fencing, which always struck me as odd, over here. More like what I'd expect to see back home. No car in the drive, no kids in the yard. No movement at all. To one side, as you came in, was a chicken run: carefully built and constructed, like everything Alan did, but now abandoned. A fox had got in, two or three times, and after the third time they gave up. Alan had got tired of cleaning up the bloody evidence of its killing and explaining it to his kids. And, I suppose, being outfoxed by a fox. The appalling part was, the fox would kill all the chickens, no matter how many, and then only take one away to eat. A killing frenzy, they called it.

I parked alongside the empty hutch, which looked like a haunted house in miniature, and got out of the car. I stood for a time beside it, listening to my engine cool, emitting that little ticking sound, like a nail on metal. The cottage, on a good day, could look quaint and cosy. Not a period cottage, so coveted in Britain, but a place of their own. The kind that Mari and I dreamed one day of having, so much more expansive than our current terrace. Room to grow, for the family to grow.

But in the mist and morning grimness it looked less lively, more dilapidated. A full-scale version of the chicken hutch. The stucco was dimpled with mould, the gutters sagged from the eaves, and in places the paint on the windows and gables had begun to crack and peel, revealing the wood beneath. Gaps showed in the shingles on the roof of the garage-turned-work-shed, where CCD had started before we moved to the larger industrial unit. The mailbox leaned at an odd angle, white like the cross on the hill, with the name 'Jones' on it. Alan Jones. Was there a more Welsh name than that? The irony being that Alan hadn't actually grown up in Wales. Not really. He'd lived most of his youth in the Midlands, in Telford, but his father was Welsh and Alan had been born there. He and Deborah had moved back when they started their family, perhaps drawn (I'm speculating) by fond memories of family holidays, or the nostalgic way his father had built up the country, the people, the culture, in his mind. The same way I will, no doubt, do with Canada for my own children. Encouraging their appreciation of ice hockey, pancakes, and tuques.

Alan was far more Welsh than me, with all those connections, but I sometimes got the impression he wasn't much more at home here. At least I had no hope or chance of ever fitting in: with my accent and my ballcap and my apologetically Canadian ways. Possibly that was why we got on, he and I, and why he needed CCD so much. He and Deborah lived away from town, didn't seem to have many local friends, and so CCD was a way to create connections, maintain human contact.

The house looked empty, and I was tempted to get back in the car, having made a token effort to do my duty. I had nothing, really, to say. Or, I didn't know what I intended to say. Escape would be a relief. A quick getaway.

But I saw the curtains twitch, a face in the window.

Deborah. In her expression I may have caught a flare of hope, before it dissolved into blankness, desolation. If so, what a cruel and unfair trick I had played. The sound of the car in the drive, when she had been waiting for two days for her husband to come home. And I was not him. I was an imposter.

I raised a hand, by way of greeting and apology, and made my way towards the house.

*

Deborah opened the door in her work clothes: long skirt, blouse, heels. That surprised me. I had expected her to be less together, somehow. Definitely not thinking about going into work. She had done her make-up, pulled her hair back in a bun and wore reading glasses with thin wire frames that I'd never seen before. A businesslike look. She ran her own web design company and had started out by using the attic in the cottage as an office, similar to the way Alan had used the garage. Around the time Alan had gone bankrupt, her business started taking off; he closed the factory and she rented a new office in town, and hired two assistants. She often had meetings in Bristol or Cardiff and the whole undertaking seemed to be doing well. Her clients ranged from start-ups and entrepreneurs to a few larger chains.

She looked at me expectantly, both fearful and hopeful of what I might have to say. I told her that I didn't have any news – worried that I was still giving false impressions – and explained I'd seen the poster, and driven out to check if there was anything I could do. She thanked me, in a controlled manner, and invited me in, though at that point I couldn't tell if she was genuinely appreciative of my presence, or merely being polite.

It was the kind of cottage where one room led on to the next with no halls or adjoining space. The living room, which we walked through, had a large hole in one wall, to reveal what had once been a boarded-up fireplace. I had helped Alan do that. The idea had been to install a wood burner, but that hadn't happened yet. Whether that was to do with lack of money, or time, or opportunity, or will, I didn't know. But it yawned there, smelling faintly of old smoke and coal dust, looking like a missing tooth. The place had quite a few jobs like that, still needing to be done. They had already put a lot of work into the house – far more than Mari and I had into ours. But then, theirs had been in a worse state to begin with, and Alan had told me that once the kids came along their energies had been redirected. Instead of adapting the house to suit them, they had adapted to suit the house.

Opposite the hole in the wall was the TV. Their children, boys of two and six, were sitting cross-legged on the floor, watching a cartoon, their faces tilted in rapture towards the screen. They were so transfixed they did not look up or take any note of me as we passed by, moving into the dining room.

Deborah explained that she hadn't sent Rhys, her eldest, to school that morning, and I said that was understandable, given the circumstances.

'I think he'll have to go this aft,' she said. 'I've missed a day and a half of work as it is, and if I miss our pitch later on we'll lose the client.'

She said this in anger, in frustration and – for no discernible reason – moved the salt and pepper shakers from the table to the sideboard.

'Sit down,' she said. It sounded like an order. 'I'll get you a cuppa.'

The kitchen was a narrow extension off the dining room, and I recalled it as having a faint mildewed scent – in the way that happens when you add double-glazed, sealed rooms to an old, damp house. I sat solemnly at the table, hands clasped, while she moved about in there, running the tap, clicking the kettle on, clattering mugs. Then, the long, percolating wait.

When I'd first started working for Alan, out of his garage, he and Deborah had invited Mari and me over for a meal. That had been four or five years back. We had sat at that same table and drunk Singha beer and eaten chicken satay and pad thai noodles and home-made spring rolls. After dinner, over coffee, they had shown us pictures of them in Thailand, sleeping in beach huts and hiking through jungles. The photos were only about ten years old (when they were about our age) but they looked much older, having been shot on 35 mm film, so soft and richly hued, saturated dispatches from the pre-digital era. Reaching out from across a temporal divide that seemed to separate us from them.

I had accepted the photos as I had accepted the meal, with gracious enthusiasm. I assumed it was a pleasant way for them to relive those days, the pre-parenthood era. It was only later that I considered the alternative, that it was a form of warning, from them to us. Enjoy what you have while you can: the best period in a relationship – the certainty and stability of marriage, without the chaos and mania of parenthood.

I could see those same photo albums – thick,

leather-bound tomes – on the shelf opposite me, but found it hard to equate that night, the fun and food and evening festivity, with the present moment, this grey and sombre morning. The discrepancy wasn't just Alan, either – and that he was missing (whatever that meant, or portended). It was us, too. Mari and I. The warning they had given us had gone unheeded. We were slipping from one life into another, just as they had. That didn't bother me so much. What bothered me was that our previous life seemed to have slid away so discreetly, unacknowledged and unmourned.

When Deborah came back, she set the tea down on the table and sat opposite me – obscuring my view of those albums – and asked me, straight out, if I knew where Alan was. She said this tightly, tersely, braced for a response, expecting me to be some harbinger with a message.

'No,' I said. 'I had no idea he was missing until I saw the poster this morning.'

She stared at me, her eye twitching. Checking for signs of dishonesty. When she found none, something went out of her. The tension of suspense. She sagged into her chair.

'You put them all up yourself?' I asked.

'The police won't,' she said dully. 'I've reported

him as missing, but there isn't much they'll do after a couple of days. Not when it's a middle-aged man.'

'When will they start taking it seriously?'

She held up both hands. 'Who knows?'

'I'm so sorry. About yesterday, I mean.'

She looked at me curiously, not even comprehending. Her eyes hollow. She likely hadn't slept much. I reminded her about calling me, about me assuring her Alan would be back soon. She shook her head, waved it away. 'It made sense at the time,' was all she said.

And it had. But of course even that emphasised the difference a day could make: between a truant husband 'sleeping it off somewhere' and this current uncertainty.

Deborah's face crumpled for a moment, and she covered it with both palms, before straightening and wiping that emotion away. She asked me how late we'd stayed at the pub. I thought about it. I had to really think – it wasn't an act – since I had been so drunk myself, and though I vaguely knew, the actual timeline had been fogged over by my lies and forgetfulness, and accuracy now seemed paramount.

'We stayed until closing,' I said. 'And after the pub had a lock-in. That went on for a while.' I paused, wondering whether to say more, to confide it all – or all that I knew. Or if I should still protect Alan. 'And I left sometime between two and three,' I said.

'I thought you'd said it was later, on the phone.'

'I was pretty hammered, but I was home before four – I know that much.'

'Were the others still there?' she asked. 'Was Branwen still there?'

She said Branwen's name in the same way that Mari had: with veiled disapproval. I admitted that she was. One strange thing I remember about my conversation with Deborah was that neither of us was drinking the tea. We both held on to the mugs, as if we needed them to communicate, but neither of us had raised them.

'But I don't think . . .' I paused, looking sideways. Out the window I could see that the yard was now overgrown, the grass collapsed under its own weight, sodden with rain. 'I don't think it's anything like that.'

'They like to flirt,' she said, almost defensively – as if I had accused *her* of being unfaithful, rather than suspecting her husband of it.

'Branwen flirts with everybody.'

'Branwen,' she said, and shook her head, as if imagining it.

I pointed out that Branwen had been the one who'd

texted me this morning, about the posters. It seemed an odd thing to do if she and Alan were shacked up somewhere. I actually used that term – shacked up – drawing on strange slang in my nervousness and awkwardness. Deborah opened her mouth to say something and then didn't, because the kids – both of them – had come into the room. Rhys was dressed in his school uniform; his brother Thomas wasn't old enough to go yet and was still in pyjamas.

'It's over, Mum,' Rhys said.

'You can put on another,' she said.

He turned and left, again without glancing at me; that was all he'd come for. Thomas lingered, boldly. He gazed at me with unblinking eyes that reminded me of a tadpole or salamander. Something about his body had that look too: still half-formed, but with all the basic structures that would become a boy, and then a man. He padded closer and did an odd, rocking dance from foot to foot: either a show of nerves or eagerness. He put his chin on the table and rested it there, then opened his mouth to speak, an action that made his whole head bob up and down, with the table providing leverage.

He said, 'Where Daddy?'

I smiled rigidly, looked to Deborah, who patted her

son's head like you might a dog, and said that Daddy would be coming home soon and encouraged him to go watch TV with his brother. But, having found a new focus, Thomas lowered himself onto the floor, cross-legged and round-bellied like a Buddha, and began to play with random toys. A few Duplo blocks, a battered matchbox car. Deborah made a rolling gesture with her hand, signalling that we could carry on. In a backwards way, it made things less awkward, having the child there.

I said, 'Could he be with somebody else?'

Deborah held up her hands, helpless. 'Not that I know of, obviously. A lot's been going on. The company, the bankruptcy. And just keeping this bloody house together. All that,' she waved, everywhere, 'with the renovations. But I assumed it would pass. I never thought...' She hesitated, then plunged on: 'I thought he might have a fling, get his end away. I never imagined him having a fully-fledged affair, running off with somebody. That requires cunning and planning.'

'Doesn't sound like Alan,' I said gently, in a way that was meant to make her smile, only it didn't. She hardly heard.

'But who knows?' she asked, then glanced down,

at Thomas. 'The kids. I never thought he'd leave the kids.'

I said it might not be that – probably wasn't that, in fact – and that he might have just needed to go away, have some time to himself. Maybe he wanted space . . .

'Or wants to separate and doesn't know how to say it.'

Mari and I had reached this same conclusion. It was hard to imagine, but less so than some of the other alternatives. I looked into my mug. It was still full. I could see my face in there – like a boy peering into a well.

'Were things that bad?' I asked.

She said she didn't think so. No worse, or better, than the relationships and marriages of their friends. 'But you never know,' she said, and looked at me in a way that seemed both accusing and a warning. Then she said, 'The honeymoon was definitely over. Let's put it that way.'

Her face folded up again, or fell away. Revealing the true strain. Not just of the past few days but the past few years. On the floor, her son was driving the toy car in lazy circles around the Duplo blocks. Watching this, I asked Deborah, 'The car. Where's your car?'

'Not at the pub.'

'If we find the car . . .'

'The police certainly won't.'

'How are you getting around?'

She said she was catching a ride into town with a friend, who would be looking after Thomas while she presented her pitch to the client. I asked what I could do to help, in that regard or anything else. She said no, assured me it was fine, and then stopped, as if considering. She put her forefingers to her temples and rubbed in circles, like a telepath.

'You could take Rhys to school,' she said. 'That would be helpful. It will mean he gets there at lunch, instead of during classes.'

'Of course,' I said.

She said she'd phone the school to tell them. 'They know about this,' she added, holding out a hand, as if gesturing to Alan, or the space he ought to have been. 'I suppose everybody does by now.'

'Have you told his family?'

'His brother. His parents are gone.'

She lowered her head, put a hand to her brow – as if shielding her eyes from a bright light. Her shoulders shook and I understood she was crying, or trying not to cry. I put my cold tea aside (I still hadn't taken

43

a sip) and stood up and made the long walk around the table, stepping over cars and plastic dinosaurs, and around the child manipulating them like a small god, and up to Deborah's chair. I put my hand on her shoulder and patted it. It was a clumsy gesture, but she reached up to squeeze my hand all the same, so fiercely I could feel her nails digging into my palms.

Movement caught my eye. Thomas had stood up and come to the table. He looked in concern at his mother, and suspiciously at me, as if I had brought all this about.

'Mummy hurt?' he asked.

Deborah's tears changed to laughter – that helpless kind of laughter. She wiped hurriedly at her eyes. 'No, baby. I'm not hurt.'

The tears had caused her mascara to run and, touching her fingers to her cheeks, she saw the black on her fingertips: smudged grains, like coal dust. She made an exasperated sound and said, 'I'm going to fix this. Watch him, will you?'

Again I had the feeling of being at fault, and maybe I was. Just by being there. Just by being a presence, in Alan's absence. I also felt the offhand way she delegated the job to me may have given me some glimpse as to how the household functioned.

Alan was not around, but, as a stand-in male figure, I would do.

Thomas seemed to take me as surrogate, too. He showed me, secretly, the town of Duplo blocks he had built, or scattered about. He said, 'It's so lovely,' in a way that made it unclear if he knew the meaning, and then proceeded to drive the car into the blocks, ruining the town, and cackled maniacally. I sat down with him and arranged the blocks in some rough order again, though what the order signified – or what he thought it signified – was also not clear. Houses? Schools? Shops? In any event, there was a pleasing simplicity to the task. We were halfway through that when Deborah came back. She had cleaned her mascara and, if anything, seemed even more restrained, more businesslike than she had before. Her heels clicked like castanets on the hardwood floor and she had a superhero schoolbag in her hand. She passed this to me and explained that Rhys hadn't done his homework, but that, given the circumstances, the teacher should understand. I was supposed to mention it, though, when I dropped him off.

Then she said, 'There's one other thing.'

I told her: 'Sure.'

'It's Alan's birthday this weekend.' She checked herself, remembering. 'But you know that.'

She meant from the night out. She said she'd ordered his present and had been waiting for the chance to pick it up from the post office.

'I know it's silly,' she said.

'No – not at all.'

'Maybe if I get him the gift, you know? Like luck.'

'I'll pick it up.'

She asked me if I might be able to put up a poster there when I stopped in, and went to fetch one for me. I ended up taking a few, and I assured her he'd be back soon, said he'd probably had a bit of a wobble (that was the term I used) and just needed to sort things out. I said I'd try to get a few people together, see if anybody knew anything. The old CCD team. I didn't mention Branwen's name, of course, but it was implied that this would include her.

Before going, I asked her, 'What's your pitch for, anyway?'

'A wine merchant's. A big company.'

'You'll be great,' I said, which seemed to startle her.

I wondered if it was exactly what Alan would have said.

*

Rhys still used a booster seat and even though his had disappeared with Alan and the family car, Deborah thought she had an old one in the garage. I helped her to look; I hadn't been in there since it had served as our workspace, back when Branwen and I were the only employees. It had one long workbench that we huddled over, by a single fan heater, and – on the opposite wall – mail-order shelving units that held various wires, boards and components.

Now, in the time since CCD had shifted base (and then closed), our former workspace had become a general storage area: the shelves filled up with old toys, filing boxes, bags of clothing and unused sports gear, including Alan's golf bag and clubs. From amid all that, Deborah dug out the booster seat. She made a dissatisfied sound: it was mouldy. The garage had damp. I remembered that. Alan and I had repaired a few shingles, but that hadn't helped. The damp was in the walls, and the floor, and you just couldn't get rid of it, Alan said.

She showed me how to install the seat, and we put a towel across it for Rhys to sit on. He seemed amenable enough, both to the idea of going to school and being driven there by me.

As we rolled back towards the reservoir, he sat quietly and gazed out his window. The angle of his seat gave his shoulders a strange hunch. He swung his legs, idly kicking at my backrest. It was irritating, but I didn't feel confident or familiar enough with him to ask him to stop.

I knew where the school was, and had been there before, on occasion. If Mari needed our car for work, Alan would pick me up on the way to the industrial unit, and such rides usually included dropping Rhys off.

I'd known Alan and his family for several years, nearly as long as I'd lived in Wales. It seemed a substantial period, though in our lives there had been little progression. Mari had her job – at a community outreach project, doing playwork with young people – and I'd done odd jobs – at a bakery, a bistro and a garage – before finding CCD. The change in us and our relationship, from early to late twenties, was negligible. Or had been until the pregnancy. But the change in Rhys, from toddler to six-year-old boy, was profound. The first time I'd seen him he'd been nearly as young as his little brother was now.

I recalled Alan telling me once that by the age of six or seven our personalities have been largely formed; at the time, I considered it interesting, a curiosity. Now, I realise he was likely thinking specifically of Rhys, who – if that were true – was essentially set in his mould: the kind of teenager and man he would become already defined, and partly determined. But I suspected it couldn't be that simple.

'Do you know where my dad went?' he asked.

He said this in the way of children: innocuous but not entirely innocent. Not naïve. Or not as naïve as we'd like to believe. I looked at him in the rear-view mirror, but he wasn't meeting my gaze: he was looking at the back of my head.

'No I don't, buddy,' I said. It seemed natural to call him buddy, as my dad had done to me and as I would no doubt do when our child came along, if it were a boy. 'But he'll be back soon. We're going to find him.'

'Maybe he's done a runner.'

He said it sneeringly, though I was unclear if he knew what it truly meant – or if he was just repeating something he had heard. Perhaps overheard, from his mother. On the phone, to friends or relatives.

'I don't think that's it,' I said.

But his sneer had already faded into puzzlement.

'But where is he running, and how far? That's stupid.'

For a moment I saw it through his eyes: the phrase interpreted literally. I had this image of Alan in trainers and tracksuit, jogging and huffing along some isolated road, his feet pounding pavement. Having abandoned the car or never having taken it in the first place. Legs extended in long, spidery strides. Eyes fixed on the horizon, determined and hopeful. It had to be true that something better lay just beyond. Then he was moving away, impressively swift, over hill and dale, majestic, as if wearing seven-league boots. A giant from a tall tale. Enveloped, eventually, by the mists.

Rhys kicked my seat, hard, as if demanding an answer.

'He'll be home,' I said.

'Tomorrow?' he said.

'Soon.'

It sounded like a lie.

'Who will drive me to school tomorrow?' he asked.

I said that I didn't know, but that – if nobody else could – I would be happy to. He did look at me, then, in the rear-view: meeting my eyes, for the first time. He seemed surprised.

'Who are you?' was what he asked.

I eased off on the accelerator. I didn't know how to answer. The question sounded accusatory and profound. I said I was a friend of his dad's, that we used to work together.

'He doesn't work any more,' Rhys said. 'He lost all our money.'

Neutrally, I said, 'That wasn't his fault.'

But again he had already moved on, his thought process slippery as water.

'Why do you talk like a cartoon?' he said.

That threw me. I had to consider what he might mean.

'I'm from North America,' I said. Then, because that didn't seem clear, I added, 'The place they make those cartoons. The land of cartoons.' This made him cackle, in a loud and maniacal way that reminded me of his brother. They both got that from Alan.

'That's silly,' he said. Then, almost shrieking: 'If you come from the land of cartoons then you aren't even real!'

He kept laughing about it for some time, periodically kicking my seat to drum it home: *You aren't even real.* And at times, over here, I had to admit it felt as if I wasn't. I existed in a state of displacement, always lost and uneasy, hovering outside 'real' life.

51

*

The school was on Lower Road, on the way out of town. Newly built, an interconnected set of squat buildings and bungalows, red-brick, with tiled roofs. Heavily fenced, in the way most schools are, now. Almost like prisons or zoos. The parking lot had barriers, but they were raised, so I was able to drive in and find a space in the visitor area. Since it was not the usual time for drop-offs or pick-ups, there were no other cars there, and no other parents around.

I opened the door to let Rhys out (he had already unstrapped himself, being used to the drill) and walked him in, feeling eerie: a combination of acting as Alan's stand-in, and getting a taste of a future life.

We went to reception, which was locked. Through the window I could see a woman sitting in an office adjacent to the entrance. I waved – unfamiliar with the system – and she looked at me blankly before buzzing us in. She came around to meet us in the foyer. I explained that Rhys was coming to school late 'because of family circumstances' (I assumed they knew about it). I passed his bag to her and said he hadn't had time to do his homework.

The woman took the bag reluctantly, as if I'd handed her a fur scarf, and drew me aside. In a lower tone – though not really so low that Rhys wouldn't have heard – she asked if he was OK to be in school.

'His mum thought it might be easier for him. Than waiting at home, I mean.'

I didn't mention the pitch, the practical reason, which seemed somehow crass.

The teacher – I assumed she was a teacher – asked, 'And what's your role in all of this?'

I hesitated, caught off guard by the veiled accusation. I had the feeling most people in the town suspected me of something, simply due to the fact I stood out so prominently. The only Canadian in town, really. Or for fifty miles in any direction.

Rhys, who had been listening closely to our exchange – our lowered voices having made no difference at all – said loudly, 'He's my mum's cartoon boyfriend!' and laughed uproariously again. I looked at him, horrified, and explained hurriedly that I was just a family friend, not a boyfriend, a work colleague of Alan's.

The teacher was actually blushing, not really believing me but pretending to accept, for the sake of decorum, what she clearly assumed to be a lie. I said something like, 'Good luck, buddy,' to Rhys, and turned to go. Only the door didn't open. The teacher had to step around me to show me a green button to press, which released the electronic lock.

'Will you be picking him up, too?' she asked.

I hesitated on the threshold, told her I didn't think so. 'But you never know,' I added, inanely.

*

When people used to ask me why I came to Wales, I would joke, 'For love.' I'd explain that I undertook an exchange year to study film at Sheffield University, as part of my undergraduate degree. I met Mari there, on a trip with the university hiking club. Our fling became a thing: after graduation I applied for a working holiday visa and came out to live in Mid Wales. At that time she had a job and I didn't – or not one that mattered – and that had decided it. It made a kind of sense at the time, even if it bewildered my friends and family. It seemed too big a commitment, for that stage of our lives. And yet there we were – or here we were – and it had worked. At least until the recession, the cutbacks: the same economic circumstances that caused Alan's bankruptcy led to Mari's outreach company having its funding withdrawn. Since then she had gotten pregnant, and I'd taken any work I could: picking up shifts back at the bakery, and also cleaning after hours at a solicitor's office. It wasn't much. It wasn't much of a life, really. We were using, and losing, our savings to get by. And the question was being asked: what are you going to do when the baby arrives? Since arriving in Wales I'd been cut off from my friends, family, and culture: lonely to the point of giddiness, but also free from troublesome questions of career advancement, bread-winning, social duty. Now, all that was rushing at us, like a train. Building speed and momentum, and totally unstoppable. At around the same time, I stopped joking about moving to Wales for love. When people asked me, I would stare at them blankly and say, 'I don't know.'

Shortly after these events – the events that I'm describing – I got a job teaching film studies at a community college in south-west England. I wasn't particularly qualified, but the school needed somebody, and immediately. Everybody – my family back home, and our acquaintances in Wales – congratulated me about the job. I had made something of myself. I could fulfil my function as husband and father. But it came with a cost: we had to leave Wales. It affected me more than I expected, seeing as Wales was the only home I'd known in Britain, but the toll on Mari was exponentially more. I can recall the moment we crossed the border, with all our belongings in our car, and Mari very heavily pregnant. I looked over at her as the Croeso Y Cymru sign withered away in the rear-view mirror; her face was positively stricken – a kind of grief I'd never be able to know or fathom. I've heard it referred to as *hiraeth*: a Welsh word for homesickness tinged with grief – though Mari would not have claimed that, or applied it to herself.

Our first child, he was born in England. That's something that troubles Mari, I know, and always will. But it just happened. Like everything else. We talk often about moving back, but that will depend on luck, on chance. On jobs, really. And even if we did move back to Wales, it wouldn't be back to our town. That's all over, now. That life, that time in our lives. And I suppose that, as much as anything, is what I'm writing about here.

*

After dropping Rhys off, I tried to call Mari and got no answer: it went straight to voicemail. That worried me. I stopped by the house, knocking and letting myself in and calling 'Hello' in that foolish way we do when not really expecting an answer. I stood listening to the sink drip before I noticed the note on the table.

Gone shopping, then for hike to reservoir. Text if you need anything. Fish and chips for dinner?

She had these impulses. What I called her pregnant impulses. It wasn't so much cravings – like we'd read about in the parenting manuals, or had been told to expect – but more like bursts of energy, sudden compulsions to act, do. I worried that she would overexert herself, that it would lead to pains and 'spotting' – those dark auguries. And all that they could portend. I texted her, reminding her to take it easy, and also explained that I was helping Deborah. Then I texted Branwen, Mike and Ellen, asking them if they could meet me at the White Lion. By way of unnecessary explanation, I added, 'About Alan. He's missing.'

Ellen – who ran a lamb farm with her second husband – said she was in the next town over, picking up supplies from Wynnstay, so couldn't make it. But Branwen said she would come, and Mike too. He wasn't working; he'd been on the dole since CCD closed.

Before heading over myself, I went to pick up Alan's birthday present at the post office opposite the Spar on the high street. It was a strange building, all stucco and concrete, circa 1960s, slightly Soviet-looking, with a red-and-yellow marquee that looked incongruous. It was near lunchtime and busy. I waited in the slow-moving line, largely made up of seniors in overcoats, boots, the occasional fedora, a few sniffling with colds. The carpet was wet from rainwater and had a muddy scent. The people in line (or in the queue) shuffled along in the accepting manner of barn animals – restless, but not impatient like me.

The walls were adorned with colourful, faded posters of exotic places, advertisements for post office bonds and accounts, and a conversion chart denoting how much local currency you could get for a pound. The Canadian dollar was sitting comfortably at £1.54, the strongest it had been in years: a resource-rich nation happily riding out the recession. The poster for Canada depicted Vancouver: the sea, the trees, the coastal mountain range. The faded colours, the strange sepia tint to the thing (it was near the window, and sun-faded), no longer looked like my city. It was just one of many – a place I could visit, or had visited at some point. I was more at home there than here, but no longer completely at home in either place.

When my turn came, I approached the counter, which was tended to by a tall, grey-haired man with a moustache stained brown from smoking. I pushed the slip Deborah had given me across the counter. I wasn't sure if you were allowed to pick up somebody else's mail, and he gazed at the slip for a long time with eyes rheumy as an old hound's. 'Alan Jones,' he said slowly, and then tilted his head up, as if searching his memory, or peering into the middle-distance, seeking to place Alan. 'Are you Alan Jones?'

I had to admit that I was picking it up on Alan's behalf. Or his wife's.

'Isn't he the bloke who's gone missing?'

'He is,' I said, staring at his bald patch, 'but we're looking for him.' As proof, I produced the poster that Deborah had asked me to put up. 'I was also wondering if I could put this on your noticeboard.'

He pursed his lips, working them around a sweet or candy of some sort that he had in his mouth. I could smell the faint minty rankness of his breath. He said, eventually, 'We're not supposed to without the person's ID, but I suppose under the circumstances...'

He was talking about the mail, not the poster. He unfolded himself from his chair and walked, with a loose, jangling gait – surprisingly limber, like a swaggering skeleton – over to the shelves of parcels and packages that they held for pick-up.

I checked my watch, used my thumb to smudge at an ink stain on the countertop. The place had gone quiet: mentioning Alan's name had drawn attention. At the next till, the other cashier (there were only two) stamped a document, passed it over to a woman in a frock coat, and an electronic voice said, in Welsh and then English, 'Till number one, please.'

The man returned, grinning eerily. Deborah hadn't told me what the gift was, and I had expected an average-size parcel. Instead, he was carrying a golf club – a driver – shrouded in bubble wrap. It was an impressive gift. Alan wasn't a good golfer but he liked it. He and I had gone to the driving range together a few times and had always talked about going more, even playing a full round, but for one reason or another it had never happened. At the range, he had hit each ball with clumsy zeal, firing them in scattershot patterns.

The postal clerk could not pass the club through the small window at his till so I had to walk around to meet him at the end of the counter, where there was a door he could unlatch and open. He also had a pack of a dozen Titleist golf balls. He handed those to me first and, before passing the club through, hefted it and examined the head and made a satisfying sound and commented on it being 'a nice club'. Then, extending it to me but not releasing it, he added, 'Well, if he doesn't come back, you can keep it.' And he laughed, a dry, harsh laugh, accentuated by the deliberate inappropriateness of the comment.

When I turned around, the line of elderly people had doubled in size – extending now almost to the door – and they were all gazing at me with what seemed to be envy and even frustration. As if I'd just won some lottery or prize draw for which I was completely undeserving. I held the club up before me, like a shepherd's crook, and made my way back through the post office towards the noticeboard; they had to part for me, some willingly, others begrudgingly, but none of them questioning the significance of my gift.

*

I was the first to arrive at the Lion. I went to the bar intending to order a coffee, but when the bartender sauntered over and asked me, sceptically, what I wanted, I asked for a pint of Carlsberg instead. Given all that was going on this was not particularly sensible, but it was what I did. I could claim that the stresses of the day were getting to me or that Carlsberg felt appropriate, being Alan's favourite drink, but if we're to be truthful (and let's face it, this story stopped being a 'story' a long time ago), then the truth is I am timid of doing anything too overtly North American, such as asking for ketchup with fries or referring to football as 'soccer' or ordering coffee in a country pub.

Also: I like to drink. There is always that. And, as of late, I had taken to drinking at odd times, away from the house, and Mari. I wasn't hiding this, exactly – she knew I did it – but it was another divide, another wedge. She could not drink and I could not give it up like some fathers-to-be do, as a way of showing support and solidarity. So I drank away from her, and pretended it was out of consideration for her, which was partly true.

At that time (just after noon on a weekday), the pub only had a handful of other patrons, including one old guy who went from pub to pub drinking a blackcurrant squash in each. He had a bowl haircut and a maroon silk handkerchief, which he used every so often to blow his nose, and the assumption was – or our assumption was, Mari and I – that he was newly on the wagon and still enjoyed visiting his old drinking haunts.

I sat on our usual sofas and poured lager down my throat in long, satisfying gulps, as if taking lungfuls of air. By 'usual' sofas I mean the ones in a small nook that Mari and I often sat in, or had done before she became pregnant. Like the old guy with his squash, we had our habits, and one of our habits was to go out to the pub on weekends and get drunk on empty stomachs and play pool on the undersized table in the corner with torn felt, and then stumble home and have sex. The next morning we would make up for the missed meal by having a large brunch of pancakes, eggs, bacon. Like the drinking, the sex had tapered off once she became pregnant. This did not come as a surprise: we'd been trained by watching romantic comedies and warned by various elders (including Alan, now that I think about it) that this would happen, but to say it was not a surprise is not the same as saying it was not missed, or not difficult, which would be a lie. I vaguely hoped that intimate aspect of our life would return to what it once was, or a close approximation, once the baby came along, but I suspected that this was a false hope. Children, family, domestic duties: I knew that all these put a strain on relationships – even if at that time I only knew it in a distant and abstract way.

I explain all this not to be crass or overly confiding but because it was on my mind, and in some ways connected to these events, and Alan, and all of this. What I had told Deborah and Mari about that night – the night of his disappearance – was true, or largely true, at least in terms of timings. But I had left out some details and of course had no real way of knowing what had transpired (the word seems unnecessarily formal) after I left. That was in part what I hoped to uncover, in calling this meeting.

The details I had left out were this: after Mari and Deborah had gone, we'd continued to drink and play quiz games and then moved to the other side of the pub to dance. I hadn't been that drunk in years – a bacchanalian level of reverie – and the end of the night came to me in fragments, flashes, bright splinters. I remembered Mike doing a shot of tequila and biting the lemon from Ellen's lips, and I remembered Alan holding onto Branwen's hips, gyrating with her in a pastiche of dirty dancing, and I remembered dipping her extravagantly and spinning her around the floor; we had switched from partner to partner until we finally collapsed on the sofas (the same sofas where I now sat) in a cloud of sweat and perfume and euphoria. I could recall Alan sitting with his arm around Branwen and staring obviously at her chest. She was wearing a red vest top and he repeatedly told her, 'Branwen – I'm feeling like a bull tonight.' And the five of us laughing uproariously. Innocent play,

surely. Or so I'd thought. And having left, I assumed
that was as far as it went, just like on the previous
nights we'd engaged in such antics – even if this time
it seemed to go that much further.

And yet. In looking back now, taking the context
into account, knowing what I know, I can't help but
perceive the atmosphere as a little more charged, a
little more desperate. And a little more pathetic. On
all our parts. Calling to mind that phrase we hear so
often growing up: you should have known better. We
should have known better.

Once I was nearly done with my pint, I got a text
from Mike. He had to go into the school because
his lad had hurt himself in the playground, so he
couldn't make our little impromptu meeting. That left
Branwen, who arrived a few minutes later. She was
wearing her blue work uniform – she worked nights
in a local care home, a BUPA centre. She was a few
years older than Mari and me, between our age and
Alan's, and wore her hair short-cropped and spiked,
tinged with red. She saw me and waved and pointed
at my glass.

'What are you having?'

If she'd asked me if I wanted another, I might have

said no. But her question didn't seem to allow for that, so I held up my glass and said, 'Carlsberg.'

She said something about fancying one herself, and went to order, chatting amicably and confidently to the bartender while she pulled the pints. I heard Branwen say, 'Isn't it strange?' and guessed they were discussing the posters.

When she came back, she put the pints on the table before us and sat next to me and crossed her legs and smoothed her skirt and started talking immediately about Alan as if she had been waiting for me, or somebody, to confide in. She told me that she'd got up and gone to buy a butty on the way to work, early, and saw the poster.

'I got your text,' I said, though of course she knew that, 'and went to see Deborah.'

'How is she?'

'Holding it together.'

'Poor thing.'

We said these words in an obligatory way; we had to say them, get them out of our system, as a kind of social etiquette. But we were both impatient to move past that phase.

Branwen took a pull of lager and put it back down – placing the glass atop the circle of condensation it had left before – and leaned towards me. In a low voice, she asked, 'Have you heard anything from him?'

'No,' I said. 'I tried texting and calling.' Then, hesitant, I added, 'What about you?'

She shook her head, no. She put her nail to her mouth and touched the edge of her lips – as if checking her lipstick. But it was only habit.

'But there's something I have to tell you,' she said.

'About the other night?'

'About the other night.' She looked towards the door. 'Who else is coming?'

I explained about Mike and Ellen and said that this was pretty much it, as far as the search party went. She didn't seem surprised.

'They probably don't want to face each other,' she said, 'in the cold light of day.'

I said OK, without really questioning or asking what she meant by that. I suspected that was all coming.

She took another sip of her pint and told me, in a long rush, that shortly after I left, the night had gotten a bit odd. That was the phrase she used: 'It all got a bit odd, then.' Firstly, Mike and Ellen had started to snog. That had happened before, even though they were technically involved with other people. 'If that's what they want to do,' Branwen said, making a distancing gesture with her hands, 'Fine, right?'

Then they'd upped and left – with each other – and Branwen had wanted to leave too, but Alan had kept talking to her, some of it nonsensical, repetitive, and much of it to do with the closure of the company, the state of his married life, the problems between him and Deborah. None of it all that unexpected. Just the things couples deal with. Just life. But all the while he had been putting his hand on her knee, her thigh. Touching her in a way that had set her on edge. As if seeing Mike and Ellen leave together had triggered something. 'Given him ideas,' was how Branwen put it.

I could imagine the scene, easily: the horrid awkwardness of it. The shift from fun, flirtatious dancing in a larger group to the creeping impropriety, misguided advances, and Branwen stuck there, feeling more and more sober as Alan became more and more drunk.

'I felt for him,' she said. 'I did. But, God – I'm not going to, you know?'

I assured her I did. Of course I did. Feeling ashamed that a small part of me, like Deborah and

Mari, suspected her – but of what? Not seducing him. Not that. I'd never really believed it. But this story – her story – I believed.

Eventually, having had enough, she'd called a cab. Alan had followed her outside to wait with her, under the pretence of being chivalrous. When she got to this part of the story, I waited glumly, ran a hand over my face – feeling the heat of my cheeks, a sense of shame and embarrassment by proxy, knowing what came next. Behind the pub, Alan had wrapped her in a goodbye hug and tried to kiss her – her neck, her face, her lips, in that order. In telling me, she giggled, anxiously, and said the kisses had been slobbery and eager, like those of some big St Bernard.

Alan had never done anything improper or lecherous or lewd before. Not that I had seen, and Branwen said something to that effect, in relating the incident. She said: 'It was so unlike him.' The counterargument might be that clearly this *was* like him, since he had done it. But that doesn't allow for the possibility that we can falter, make mistakes, do something 'out of character' – and that this might have been an instance of that. Whether it played out exactly in the way Branwen had told me, I can't be sure, but if anything,

I'd suspect her of softening it, as a way of sparing Alan the full force of disgrace. And I'd be lying if I said it didn't lessen him, somehow, in my mind. The pettiness and the smallness – the gross and hopeless fumbling. It wasn't the impulse that offended, but how he'd given in to it. That loss of control. Wasn't that something they said, in the old days – and might have said the generation previous, in a town like this? *He couldn't control himself. He'd lost control.* But maybe it was more than that, too. More than a burst of lust, a lapse in judgement, an act born of desperation – a hapless urge, like some dog that leaps on the leg of a passer-by, whining with sexual frustration. Maybe Alan wasn't just groping and clinging to Branwen but – through her – to something else.

Which hadn't made it any less grotesque. She'd pushed him off, angled away. 'Jesus Christ, Alan,' was what she'd said, and I felt like saying the same, in hearing all this. *Jesus Christ. Get it together. Get a hold of yourself.* She assured me there was no sense of threat, and then added, 'I can take care of myself.'

When the cab came, she'd tried to get him to ride with her – so it could drop him off after her. But Alan had refused, out of humiliation or wounded pride, or a kind of childish petulance. He'd said he was going to sleep it off, in the back of his car. Go home in the morning.

'I made him promise not to drive,' she said, sounding worried. Defensive, even. 'But what if he did?'

I had already thought of that, before hearing her story. It wasn't uncommon in town, in most small towns – where there was no public transport. I'd done it. Most of us had done it. It wasn't a matter of not driving drunk, but of not driving when you were too drunk.

'Somebody would have seen,' I said. 'Or found him.'

'Sure,' she said.

She had stopped drinking amid the torrent of story, and now she reached for her pint, taking a long pull. I did the same, nearly finishing mine. When I put the glass down, I stared dully at the wall opposite us – decorated with brown and green bottles, all filmed with dust – and I thought of how Alan might have been feeling, lying in the back of his car, under an emergency blanket, as early morning crept up on him, in the parking lot at the back of the White Lion, having harassed and made a failed pass at a friend and colleague.

71

'Say he did sober up,' I said, and stopped. Something else had occurred to me. 'He wakes up, but doesn't want to go home. He's feeling guilty. Can't face Deborah.'

'But nothing actually happened,' Branwen said. 'He didn't cheat on her.'

I said he'd tried, though. He'd tried and failed, which, in a way – perversely – might have made him feel worse (I didn't say that to Branwen). An impotent cheat. Worthless. The thought so diminishing. All of the immorality of infidelity, but none of the satisfaction.

'He might not have been ready to go back,' I said, 'and figured he'd go someplace to recover, pull himself together.'

Branwen snapped. 'Unit 31.'

'That's it.'

Alan had occasionally slept at the CCD industrial unit before, back when we were slammed with work. And, a few times, after a particularly rowdy staff do. The unit was on the outskirts of town, and much closer than their cottage. Easier to get to, half-drunk and half-sober, than the long drive around the reservoir and up the hill and along the back roads and lanes to their cottage. I hadn't thought of it at first, since the place hadn't been on my mind since the company's closure. But it was still there, and hadn't been rented out again. The units on the estate had very little occupancy, due to the recession, the lack of business loans, the lack of interest and support.

'We should go,' Branwen said.

'Do you have work?' I said, since she was in uniform.

'I worked the early shift – I just got off.'

'I should be OK to drive,' I said.

'You're fine.'

'I definitely haven't had as much as Alan,' I said – a comment that should have been inappropriate, but which made us both laugh uproariously. Partly, it just felt good to have a plan, to be doing something, rather than nothing. And to know that somebody – us – cared enough to look for him, despite his flaws, despite his failures, despite his fumbling misdeeds and indecent advances. I took comfort in that: you couldn't simply walk away, vanish, disappear as easily as he seemed to have done. Your wife might still go to work and your kid might still go to school and your golf club might still arrive in the mail and your life might still carry on – only without you in it – but at least somebody would be looking for you.

*

Before driving over, we put a few more of Deborah's posters up, in any of the places she had missed: the chippy, the bookshop, the pub itself. There was no real point to this – by then word must have gotten around – but it made us feel proactive and product-ive. We were going to meet back at my car, and as I walked, I phoned Mari. I didn't expect her to pick up – the reservoir only had intermittent coverage – but she did. Her voice sounded distant and even though there was no background noise there was a sense of her being outside, of the vastness of surrounding space. She was also breathing heavily. I asked where she was, and she said on the trail that ran down one side of the reservoir – opposite the cross – and up to the tourist information area and café.

'You OK?' I said.

'I'm fine.'

'Take it easy.'

'Exercise isn't dangerous. It's good for bean.'

She had taken to calling this baby bean, too. It made me uncomfortable because, in my head, the name was spoken for. But I never said as much. It was her right, and her baby – so much more than mine.

'I called the CCD team,' I said. 'We're going to check out our old place, on the industrial estate.'

She asked why, and I tried to explain. Taken out of context, it sounded a little silly – grasping at straws. A way of making myself feel useful, like the posters. But at least she seemed to accept it. I wanted to remind her to be careful again, but knew it wouldn't go down well, so instead I jokingly told her to keep an eye out for Alan. As if he might be hiding behind a rock or a tree, leprechaun-like, at the reservoir.

Then we hung up. She hadn't asked who I was with, and I'd neglected to mention Branwen. It seemed an extraneous detail, and I hadn't wanted to have to explain, laboriously, how she and I had ended up as the only members of our quasi-search party.

I don't know what it was about Branwen that gave rise to these seeming suspicions. Perhaps, simply, that she was attractive – she had classic features and looked a little like an ageing starlet, somehow, who had gotten happily stuck in a small town – and she carried herself with the easy confidence of a person used to drawing attention and who had a compelling effect on others, particularly men. Yet, it seemed odd to assume that just because of that she was somehow a threat: to relationships, to marriages, to stability. Odd, and unfair.

But still: I understood. There was a clear difference between, say, the way Branwen flirted and the way Deborah or Mari might. She liked to dance and drink and tease and laugh, and did those things without restraint, with an impish sense of imperviousness. So maybe it was a jealousy of that, rather than a real anxiety over her influence. She was not as repressed as the rest of us, when it came to the workings of the heart, and the body. She spoke openly, and often in outrageous ways, about relationships, sex, and sexual antics. She had, for example, told us that she'd posed naked when younger for her boyfriend photographer, who'd then sold the pictures to a magazine – perhaps one of those British lads magazines. A phenomenon that I'd always found bewildering, there being no real equivalent back home. She told the story with neither pride nor embarrassment, but rather with a sense of absurdity, a kind of 'Would you believe it?' tone. The same tone, I suppose, we might use to tell a story about doing something silly at a party or getting in a drunken altercation, or any of the other foolish things we do in our youth.

A kind of brazen confidence. That's what she had, what made her so compelling. And, it has to be said, it's one of the things I miss about her. I haven't seen Branwen for years. We received a card, I think, when the baby was born. The first one. By then we had moved away. She and I must still be friends on Facebook, and I could find her, perhaps, among all the other digital ghosts. But of course I never do, just as I'm sure she never bothers looking at my page, wondering what I'm up to. And yet, next to Mari and Alan, she was the person I knew best, and felt closest to at that time.

*

It wasn't until Branwen and I met back up at my car that I remembered the golf club, which was propped up on the passenger seat. I moved it into the back, explaining to Branwen about having to pick it up for Deborah, and what had happened when I'd dropped Rhys at school.

'Now the whole town will think she and I are having an affair.'

Branwen, settling into the seat, made a dismissive gesture. 'I'm supposed to have had affairs with half the men in this bloody town.' Then, after a beat, she added, 'Some of them I have, to be fair,' and cackled, delighted, in that way of hers, as I pulled out onto the high street.

I had a cosy buzz from the lager and drove with

a sense of focus now that we had a practical goal in mind.

Branwen put the radio on and sat with her purse on her lap and an upright posture, the pose of an elderly lady riding the bus. She began to snap her fingers along to the music, and said, 'Oh – I like this song, I do.'

I remember that well, and fondly: the way she spoke, the peculiarity of adding 'I do' to the end of a sentence. I don't know if that is Welsh, or British. Mari doesn't do it, and it's definitely not Canadian. Perhaps it's the equivalent of 'eh?' for us – something I never really said, until I came here and people seemed to expect it of me. So it became a habit.

The industrial unit was on the east side of town. We had to drive along the high street, and up to the roundabout at the bypass. The bypass was a stretch of blacktop that ran along the route of the old train tracks, passing the station house, which had now been turned into a hot tub and Jacuzzi dealership and, next to it, a hardware sales and repair shop. The train line and station had been closed back in the sixties, and I'd been told the same was true for many small towns in Wales. The closure had hurt business, and the bypass, which was more recent, had exacerbated that for all the usual reasons. If tourists could stop off at the Texaco and Costa and Burger King next to the bypass, they didn't need to venture into town for those supplies.

All those changes had occurred before Mari and I had arrived, but our neighbours still recalled earlier, livelier times. We had no such points of comparison. For us, the town had always been sleepy, sedated, somewhat comatose. A strange place to spend our twenties, we both agreed. Shouldn't we be in a city, a cultural centre? And yet we'd stayed. We'd stayed – like so many people in small towns – because we could and had no reason to leave. Which sounds unduly negative, but in reality we were content. She had her career in playwork, which did not pay well but was her passion, and I had my various odd jobs, and no real pressure to succeed, or achieve. It equated to a kind of happiness, and an existence free from the stresses we live with now.

The industrial estate was a few miles down the road, on the other side of the bypass. It wasn't until we were nearly there that something else occurred to me.

'If he did come out to the factory,' I said, 'he probably wouldn't still be here.'

'Even if he slept it off, it's been another full day.'

We rolled on in silence, thinking about that, as blacktop scrolled beneath the tyres.

'Unless he's hiding out,' I said. I imagined Alan crouched among all the detritus of his lost business, gone AWOL, like an old soldier returning to the barracks, unable to handle 'real' life, after the good cause was gone. Returning instead to the place where he felt safest. We would approach and he'd call out to us and tell us to stop right there: that's far enough.

'Or stayed the night,' she said, 'then went someplace else.'

'Or did something else.'

Branwen looked at me, startled. I must have had glimmers of the thought a few times throughout the day. But always I'd skirted around it, pushed it aside. Now, something about approaching the industrial estate, and the thought of Alan there, made it seem more plausible.

'Like what?' Branwen asked.

I just shrugged and put on my blinker. The turn to the estate was coming up, and a small sign: *Cartref Industrial Estate*. Cartref. I'd worked there for a year or two before I'd learned – from Mari – that it was the Welsh word for home.

'God,' Branwen said, 'he can't have . . .'

'Topped himself?'

I posed it as a question. It was the only way I could say it – as if it were rhetorical. And it had to be that phrase, that odd British phrase, which made it more palatable, almost comical. Not killed himself or committed suicide, but topped himself. Like popping the top off a bottle.

'He can't have,' she said, pulling a pantomime 'aghast' face. 'Done *that*?'

I knew what she meant, that it seemed unthinkable, but it hit men, at this time of life, didn't it? I'd read that somewhere. That the highest suicide rate wasn't among teenagers, like I had always assumed, but middle-aged men. The dark side of the mid-life crisis. You could buy a sports car or have an affair or change jobs or do yourself in. That was another way of putting it, also easier to say than killing yourself. Do yourself in. As easy as turning in for the night, but for ever.

'No,' I said. 'Not Alan.'

'He's the last person . . .' Branwen said.

But she trailed off, not finishing. Perhaps realising that it was what people always said about suicides. And if I was honest, Alan's jocular friendliness and forced good cheer had a brittle, fragile quality to it. An eggshell, concealing another Alan. And then there was his behaviour, the thing with Branwen. The Alan I knew – the 'Alan' we were talking about – would never have done that, either. So we were already in the realm of unthinkable actions, of previously un-imagined possibilities.

Still, it was a long way from that drunken mis-demeanour to suicide. To the thought of us going to the unit and not finding evidence of Alan having been there, or Alan hiding out, but Alan's body. His remains. Hanging from the rafters, or slumped in a chair. I'm fairly sure Branwen was thinking similar thoughts as we wound our way through the industrial estate. It consisted of four rows of six units, linked brownstone structures with shingled roofs. We had been one of the first companies to move into the units. That had been when we'd begun receiving orders from Europe, China and the Middle East. We'd worked long days and nights and Alan paid us overtime and implemented perks and bonuses for hitting production targets. It had almost started to feel like a real job. Then came the slowdown, the recession. The withering time. Clients who couldn't pay and orders that were cancelled. And pay cheques that had to be delayed. Alan had taken out further small-business loans to keep us afloat. Nobody was formally fired: Alan just trimmed down our shifts, and we'd all had other jobs on the side we could turn back to. Ellen had the farm, I had the bakery, Branwen had the care home. By the time the end came it was expected, inevitable. Like pulling the plug on a terminal case.

Most of the other units had never been rented, or had only been temporarily leased by companies that went the same way as CCD. Ours was on the end: Unit 31. Alan had chosen it because the number was the reverse of bad luck: 13. It had a shuttered garage door and a regular access door – both closed, of course. Alan's car wasn't out front, but it was possible he had opened the garage door and driven in so as not to attract attention.

I parked out front and turned off the engine. Branwen and I sat for a moment, and she admitted she was worried about what we'd find.

'It will be fine,' I said. 'He won't have done it here.'

The words sounded wrong: as if I now believed he *had* done it, only somewhere else.

We got out and together approached the garage door. Alan had never asked us to turn in our keys:

it hadn't seemed to matter, since nobody else was using the unit. Mine was still on my keychain – one of my keepsakes, or mementos. I'd had the secret, comforting thought that I could always go back, like Alan may have done, like we were about to do now. I crouched to unlock the door, and the two of us worked our hands beneath the sill, pulling up together in a well-practised motion. It was weighted, so once it reached a certain point it became easier, continuing under its own momentum.

We peered into the dark. It was a large space – perhaps the size of a pool hall – and amid the clutter and shadows it was hard to make out much. Impossible to tell if there was a body slumped amid all the refuse and remnants.

'Bloody hell,' Branwen said and marched in and hit the light switch, just inside. Only, the lights didn't come on. The power had been shut off.

'Alan?' I called. 'You here, man?'

Nothing but silence. I knew where the power box was – on the outside of the unit – from having to reset it when Alan and I tripped a breaker while using his chop saw. I told Branwen I'd see if I could get it switched on, and walked around to the back.

The box was closed but not properly locked – it

was sitting half on its latch – and I took hope from that. I thought it might mean Alan had been there. I popped it and swung it down on its hinge and flipped the main breaker to 'on'.

'That did it,' Branwen shouted.

When I walked back around, she'd made her way into the centre of the space. It hadn't changed since the day we'd closed. The overhead tube lights flickered and hummed, casting a white pallor across shelves still laden with electrical components and wires and a set of circuit boards in the middle of the floor (the last job we'd been working on, which never got finished or delivered to the client). There was all that, but no Alan, and no body.

I pulled down the shuttered door, mostly out of habit, and went to join Branwen. We looked around together, making comments about it bringing back memories, and then she grabbed my bicep in a way that startled me and pointed to the workbench and said, 'Look!'

On the worktop the plates and cups and plastic glasses from our closing party were still laid out, under a banner that we'd intended to be humorous but now seemed grim and depressing: RIP CCD. We walked that way and studied the remnants: paper plates and a few stale pretzels. Among them stood three empty Prosecco bottles, and another that was half-full. Branwen held that one up, tilted it, and – as if conducting a lab experiment – poured out a glass. It fizzed. She looked at me, surprised, and tried a sip.

'He must have opened it,' she said.

'He was here.'

I went to check the toilets – two cubicles, empty, the bowls going brackish with rust and stagnation, smelling faintly of fish tanks – and then the office, Alan's office, which he'd partitioned off from the main floor of the factory. He wasn't in there either (I didn't really expect him to be), but the office felt warm. Beneath the desk was a small electric heater and it had come back on with the power. I lingered, poking about. The desk and floor were littered with papers, and draped over the chair was a packing blanket – the kind we'd often wrapped shipments in. Alan had used it as a makeshift duvet, I suspected, while he'd slept.

I went through the papers. They were mostly old orders and receipts and bills and unpaid notices, warnings of fines and foreclosures. I couldn't tell if Alan had gone through them the previous night or if they'd simply been lying about from when we'd closed. Some seemed less dusty than others, so I thought they might have been perused, disturbed. I felt like a detective from the dime-store novels I'd read, growing up. But, of course, I didn't find any evidence of doctored figures, or embezzled funds. The thought now seemed absurd.

Still, I did find a clue. In moving some of the papers, I noticed a phone. Alan's phone. It was off, which made sense – Deborah would have tried to call him, many times. I picked it up and turned it on. It had charge. A cheap Android phone without a lock or keycode. It showed several messages – voicemails and texts – pending. I checked the texts and saw several from Deborah, and my own. But there weren't any from somebody else, from some mystery woman. I didn't look at them, or listen to the voice messages. I could imagine what Deborah might have said: her messages angry and frustrated and then, increasingly, worried, concerned, fretful. *Where are you? What are you doing?* And pleading. *Please come home. Please call. The kids miss you. I don't know what to tell them.*

I scanned his recent calls, but he hadn't made any for the past two nights. Then, after a moment's hesitation, I opened his browser and checked the history. I thought I might find further evidence of him contemplating suicide: those insidiously helpful sites detailing the best ways to go about it. I didn't find anything like that, but late the night before (or early yesterday morning), he'd visited some porn sites with lewdly ridiculous names. I cleared the browser and pocketed the phone. It made a kind of wretched sense. He'd made a bungled pass at Branwen, possibly slept in his car for a bit, and driven out here and continued to drink Prosecco left over from our closing down party, then jerked off amid bills and notices and warning citations. Maybe used some of them to clean up. Maybe fell asleep for a time in the chair, with a boxing blanket for warmth.

I flicked out the office light, and in the shift to shadow I fancied I caught a glimpse of Alan – as if the blanket had taken on his shape. A kind of shadow-version of him, looking at me, forlornly resigned.

*

On the other side of the factory floor Branwen had taken her old seat on what we called 'the assembly line', though it was essentially a workbench with three high chairs. She had topped up her glass of Prosecco and filled another for me. She'd also turned on the battered stereo we kept there. Alan had cleared out his computer and any valuable electronics, but left the junk for the bailiffs, who'd never bothered to claim it. Maybe they'd been made redundant, too. Maybe we were all outmoded, obsolete.

As I approached, I saw that Branwen was working. Or rather, she was going through the motions of work. She'd taken a circuit board from one of the leftover boxes and begun inserting transistors, diodes and integrated circuits: the kind that looked like little insects. Within the company we'd all had our jobs and that had been one of hers. From the beginning, I'd often worked alongside Branwen on the assembly line. So it seemed natural for me to take up position next to her, in the adjacent chair. She smiled at me, and we held up our glasses of Prosecco, touching the rims together. They were cheap plastic tumblers that 'clicked' instead of 'clinked', but the effect was satisfying.

'To Alan,' we both said.

The toast was buoyed up by hope, by the newness of our discovery. We had not found him, yet, but we had found evidence of him. We would be able to report back to Deborah that Alan had slept here. He had stayed for a while, sobering up (I told Branwen about the office, but not about the porn). Then, maybe, he had driven off 'to get his head together' or to 'figure some things out'. Phrases like those sounded safe, familiar, and quite positive, quite plausible. It could be that when I went to deliver the golf club, his car would be in the drive. The scare would be over, and it would all take on the security of being in the past.

I savoured those thoughts and sipped my Prosecco, the sour bubble-burst, and put it aside. I dug out an old soldering iron and plugged it in. While it heated up I unwound a coil of tin-lead solder, and Branwen passed me the first of the boards she had prepared: a single-sided PCB, made out of the usual green fibre-glass. When the iron was hot enough I aligned the tip with a transistor and touched the solder to it. The metal smoked and liquified and sealed the transistor in place. From there I moved on to the next component, and the next. The layout of the board was familiar – it was for an oscillating fan – and it all came back easily, like muscle memory retained from playing an instrument. Branwen and I fell into our old, familiar rhythms. She had turned the heater on and it glowed beneath the counter, scalding our knees and shins. Left over from the party was a bowl of hard candies, twisted up in plastic wrappers, and between sips of Prosecco we sucked on them. They'd gone a little soft, a little chewy, but retained their flavour – that pungent peppermint that almost burned.

Branwen swayed along to the music, moving without self-consciousness. We didn't mention the oddness of it, the uselessness of sitting there, creating circuit boards that would never fulfil their purpose. She prepped each one and passed it to me and when I finished I would put it aside, turning to the next. It felt quite ordinary, perhaps because the point of such tasks had always been fathomless to us: only Alan had any real sense of what the components did, or how the boards functioned in the devices they were designed for. We simply made them, the work reassuringly repetitive, satisfyingly Sisyphean. When we finished one, we'd move on to the next, assuming – with blind faith – that there would always be more, and that had been the case. Until it wasn't, and we'd had to return to our other, equally repetitive jobs.

Unlike Branwen and me, Alan hadn't found or done any other work, as far as I knew, since the closure of CCD. He'd stayed at home, looking after the kids, and he was good at that.

'Do you think we should call Deborah?' Branwen asked.

'I could tell her when I drop off the golf club.'

'Might be better in person.'

'He might already be home.'

'Or will be soon. Where else could he go?'

We both considered that, and Branwen took a sip of her Prosecco. Slowly, feeling my way towards the thought, I said he might have driven off, gone away someplace.

'To break up with Deborah,' she said.

I touched iron to solder, melting metal, completing the circuit.

'She's worried about that,' I said, 'but it could also be something else. I mean, those guys who get up one day and . . . leave.'

She looked at me curiously. 'Where?'

'Anywhere. They just walk away: from their jobs, their kids, their wives, everything. Maybe leave the country. Go to Europe, or to America. A kind of breakdown or whatever.'

'God,' Branwen said. And I expected her to say something about that being terrible, but instead she said, 'Wouldn't that be brilliant? Just imagine. Where would you go?'

'Paris.'

'New York.'

'Tokyo.'

'Casablanca.'

We kept on like that, coming up with more and more exotic places. Until Branwen said: 'We should do it.'

'Let's get in my car right now.'

'Drive to Portsmouth.'

'Where do ferries go from there?'

'France.'

She topped up our glasses, emptying the bottle, and we toasted again: the problem of Alan forgotten, obliterated by this new dream. When Branwen finished drinking, she sighed and let out a small, delicate hiccup. 'I wish we really could go away.'

It sounded like a fairy tale: the moment it could become reality. Wishing the dream into existence. I could feel the purr of the heater on my legs and hear the fizz of bubbly in my glass, simmering.

'One day,' I said. 'Some day.'

And Branwen checked her watch, and said, 'God, I'm bursting.'

She scurried across the floor, latched the door to the loo behind her. I put the remainder of my Prosecco aside. I was on the cusp of not being able to drive. Not safely, anyway – which in truth hadn't always stopped me before. I took our old plastic kettle to the big washbasin, adjacent to the loos, and rinsed it several times. Then I refilled it and plugged it in and shouted to Branwen, asking if she wanted a cuppa.

'Please!' she called back, and flushed.

The kettle was reaching a boil, so I didn't hear her coming up behind me. She slid her arms around my waist and leaned against me. She had done things like that before, of course. The intimacy of the CCD family. But it had always been with the others around. Was this any different? I didn't think so. She had her chin on my shoulder, and she was still humming faintly to the radio. Nothing more than her usual charms. As careless and meaningless to her as our daydream of Europe, of running away.

Or maybe it was more than that. Maybe I could have turned to face her and taken her in my arms and kissed her. Ravishing and impassioned as a romance novel. And I might even have done it. If I had been sure, certain of the signals. Or if I'd been another type of person. Less timid, less dutiful, and more lustful. Or more drunk, like Alan. But of course that had been his mistake. Poor Alan, with his bankrupt company and his unpaid bills and misguided come-ons, all the ongoing rejections, amounting to the same thing.

I wasn't like that, like him.

Still. The impulse was there, the possibility of

transgression. And so I did something eccentric, as is my tendency in charged situations: like an actor trying to break out of role. I placed my hands over hers and began to sway, picking up the rhythms of her body, feeling the music through it. And then I raised our arms and spun extravagantly towards her, adopting a formal, waltzing pose: hand to hip, and palm to palm, straight-backed and straight-faced. Branwen didn't baulk at all. She played her role, too. We sashayed and twirled around like that, drunk enough to commit to the performance and sober enough to see the absurdity: a queen and jester dancing in the ruins of somebody else's kingdom. And we put on a good show, in that moment. A skilful double act.

Until the song ended, and the DJ came on, prattling away, and we stepped respectfully apart. I mock-bowed and poured the tea and we sat on our stools by the heater and cupped our mugs and took big, scalding slugs, sobering up, rousing ourselves from the faint feeling of wonder.

*

Was it really so romantic, how it transpired, our little flirtation in the factory? Likely not. I doubt Branwen even remembers it, now. But the dancing happened, and the closeness, and the sense of possibility. Without any awkwardness. I felt easy and comfortable with her as we left the place, shutting it down again, for the last time. Turning off the heater, the radio, the lights, the kettle, pulling down the garage door together, and flipping off the breaker.

The shock of the outdoor cold, the dim strangeness of twilight. All of it like a dream of reality. And us climbing into the car, like old partners. We didn't talk much on the way back, but the silence was affable, familiar. I asked Branwen if she wanted me to take her home, but she said I could drop her at The Kings, a pub a little further along from the Lion. Her new work colleagues would be there. 'I've got a taste for it now,' she said.

I smiled. 'You always have a taste for it.'

'Shush, you.'

'Wish I could join you,' I said, but it was a token comment. 'I ought to get this golf club to Deborah, though, tell her about Alan.'

'I hope he's there.'

'I'll let you know.'

But I no longer felt as hopeful as I had inside the factory, when his presence had been close, in the vicinity. If I had, I might have tried calling. I didn't want to know, yet. It would last longer if I drove.

At The Kings there was a parking spot right by the door, so I pulled up, like a carriage driver, and Branwen gathered her bag and let herself out. We made plans to meet again, have a drink sometime – softening the goodbye with those ministrations – and she slung her bag around her shoulder and walked to the door and held up a hand, waggling her fingers at me by way of goodbye without really looking back, knowing I'd be watching.

Before heading out to Deborah and Alan's, I decided to phone home. Partly to remind myself I had a home. Partly to absolve myself of the sense of straying, of low-level philandering. To banish the thoughts of factory dancing, of running away – from my wife, my unborn child, the life that was coming at me.

Except, when I got my phone out I saw I had messages – three of them. I felt a chill, a crawling, deep in my guts. Guilt giving way to fear. They were all texts from Mari, telling me to come to the reservoir, asking to be picked up. There was also a voicemail. I dialled the number to listen, put it on speaker and dropped it on the passenger seat – listening while making a U-turn in the middle of the high street. Her message was short, terse: asking where I was, saying she needed me to come to the reservoir. Needed: that was the word she used.

I downshifted and hit the gas, feeling shaky and electric, anxiety flushing the booze from my system. I circled the roundabout and headed out of town towards the reservoir, retracing my route from that morning. Only it was dusk now, and the November mist had darkened into a smoke-like haze. I put on my fog lights and negotiated the curves around the lead mines, up the long incline past the dam, and the steeper grade overlooking the reservoir. The thought of it happening now, again, when I'd been gallivanting around with Branwen, having my little dance, on a wild goose chase for Alan, was too horrifying to accept. The punishment was too severe, the repercussions too brutal and harsh. Life wasn't like that. I didn't deserve that. And Mari. To be on her own.

The hill was steepest near the top: the nose of my car angling up, so that gravity and acceleration seemed to pull me back into my seat. Such foolishness, given the road, and the circumstances. In my memory, I see myself coming very close to real peril, but it might not be as close as I now imagine. This much is true, at least: I was speeding, and half-cut, and panicked. Even so, I remembered the hairpin in time – just a second before the flowers and roadside shrine emerged from the haze, the cross white as a lighthouse beacon, warning me. I was braking by then, decelerating, but the turn was still intense, sickeningly risky.

I pulled out of it and slowed to a crawl, stunned, trundling into the parking lot of the café as if at the tail end of a rollercoaster ride. My neck hairs prickling, my stomach queasy from the after-surge.

I parked up – the lot only had three vehicles in it – and ran, jacketless, through the cold to the café. Only one customer was inside, at a table near the windows. Mari. She was watching the parking lot, looking out for me, and I shoved open the door and crouched by her and put a hand on her knee and asked if she was OK. Looking back, I realise she probably wanted to be angry with me, for not returning her texts, but my behaviour was so dramatic that she had to respond.

'I'm OK,' she said, looking bewildered. 'A little tired. Where have you been?'

'I got your message. You said you needed me.'

She nodded, mystified by my urgency, explained that she had seen something, on her walk, that might be important. I had to listen carefully. I was having a hard time following.

'What about bean?'

She put her hand there. Her belly looked bigger, sitting down. Bean was fine, she said. But she was glad I'd come. She needed to show me what she'd found.

'Sure, sure,' I said, already trying to pretend I was OK with this – and knowing I would never tell her about the extent of my terror, the mad rush to the reservoir. The close call. 'Let me just get a coffee or something – you want anything?'

'No – it's outside ...'

She pushed back her chair, ready to stand, but I pointed to the counter imperatively.

'I just need a coffee first, OK?'

Before she could say anything else I turned and walked mechanically to the till. Fortunately, the worker was in the kitchen, doing dishes. I was able to stand on my own for a moment, assembling my social face. On the wall behind the shelves was a painting by a local artist – an impressionistic green and blue landscape of the reservoir, the hills. I stared at it. It could have been any reservoir, really. Any place in Wales.

When the worker came back – an elderly woman with her hair done up in a bun – I ordered an

Americano, which she made from the machine behind the counter, doing it with the seriousness and gravitas of a real barista, even though it was an automatic machine with a digital display: the same kind you might put a pound in at a truck stop, or rest area.

I paid and took a sip before carrying it back to Mari. She had stood up anyway, still impatient to take me outside. I didn't argue. I didn't want to argue with her about anything, ever again. I went ahead of her and held open the door and hovered nervously behind her, like a sentry or guard, as she led me across the parking lot. She walked me to the edge of the lookout, at a waist-high stone wall, and told me to look.

'I got here,' she said, 'and I was just sitting, having my tea.'

I assumed what she had to show me was one of her characteristic hiking discoveries: a red kite nest, or distinct rock formation, or an unobtrusive mound that might have once been a motte-and-bailey castle or iron-age hill fort. She had a knack for noticing the landscape.

'That's when I saw it,' she said, tensely.

I stared, clueless, and sipped my coffee and took in the view of the reservoir at dusk. From there I could see the whole thing, up to the top of the dam, where the water ended abruptly, surreal and unnerving. I could see, too, the lonely beacon of the cross, glowing through the haze. I told Mari I didn't know what she wanted me to notice, so she pointed.

'There – under the cross.'

Below it on the steep hillside I had the impression of strips, running down the slope. Like the lines left when you cut grass. I straightened and took a step closer and peered into the murk, as if I could telescope or magnify my vision. The markings looked like the tyre tracks of a vehicle, and I vaguely remembered seeing such tracks, after the family had gone into the water. But that had been months ago. Nearly a year. It couldn't be the same tracks.

I placed my coffee cup atop the wall and turned to Mari. Neither of us said anything – nothing at all. As if saying anything could make the possibility real, or make her discovery vanish, mystically, before we had the chance to verify it. We just got into the car together. I left my coffee where I'd put it down and reversed out of my parking spot.

A Dwr Cymru access road snaked down from the tourist information spot to the reservoir. We eased past the no access sign and manoeuvred around a series of steeply descending switchbacks. About three quarters of the way down, a black-and-yellow traffic barrier blocked our path. Beyond it, the road became unpaved, rough-hewn track. I got out and Mari got out, too. I said I didn't think she should come.

'I'm fine.'

'It's getting dark, and it's rocky, and not even a trail. Stay here.'

We stared at each other. I hadn't said it nastily, but she could see something in my face – the residual fear showing there. And the fear that had haunted me since our first loss. Besides the terrain, I didn't know if it would be good for her to witness what we might find.

'OK,' she said.

I walked, keeping the hill and cross in sight on my right. The gravel road crunched wetly underfoot. The mist was thicker here, lying low over the water. The opposite side of the reservoir was invisible, blotted out by cottony haze.

The track ended at a testing station of some sort – a little hut – and from there I was able to scramble down to the beach. I say 'beach', but it wasn't a beach. Not really. The reservoir was like many others in Wales: created from streams that had been dammed, often drowning farms, villages and towns. So rather than sand, the shore was made up of mud and gravel and stone. The occasional rotten tree-stump, or remnants of a stone fence. And a foetid stench. I walked along, under the hill and cross, scanning the ground.

It wasn't hard to find the tracks Mari had spotted from the lookout. They were there. They were real. Up close – especially by the shore – they were obvious. At another time of year, they would have been noticed immediately. In midsummer, the reservoir was filled with fishing skiffs, rowboats, sailboats, and the shorelines crawled with hikers and scout groups. But boating season was over, the marina locked. So the tracks had remained there, waiting to be found, by the first person who had looked: who had really looked, in the way Mari did, whenever she surveyed landscapes and terrain. All my own searching had been misguided, errant, off-track entirely. But, somehow, she had found this.

The tracks ran straight down the hill – from the cross, which was now obscured by the angle of the landscape – and into the water. The hill was straight and steep, a scarp slope, with at least a seventy-degree gradient. Just a long fall, with your wheels skimming the ground, the world sliding away from you. Juddering around in your seat, head rebounding between the seatback and wheel. I stared up there, my whole body tense, remembering my own turn.

I walked to the edge of the water, standing right between the tracks. The reservoir was still and waveless, as unnatural and artificial as a pane of glass. On the surface I saw the reflection of dull, tarnished sky – like old pewter. The hill behind. In the foreground stood a figure, a shadow. A watery mirage version of myself. And beyond that, beneath it, a car bumper. Tail lights. A licence plate. Submerged, but only by a few feet. The rest of the car was deeper, and obscured, but the colour was familiar. I had the thought that I would dive down; I even waded out a few steps, up to my calves. But I stopped. What was the point? I retreated to shore and sat for a time, hunched down on a rock, feeling the cold of the water in my jeans, my socks and shoes. Like I was sitting with my feet in blocks of ice. I wonder now if that was shock, if that was what shock feels like.

But I didn't feel panicked or addled. I suppose I was trying to mourn, to pay my respects. Even so, I understood that was a temporary state. We would have to make calls. To the emergency services first.

Then Deborah. Should it come from us? I wasn't sure. I didn't have my phone, anyway: it was in the car. I trudged back to get it, dripping and feeling the squelch of sodden socks in my shoes. It was only about a ten-minute walk.

Mari must have known. She must have guessed by the way I was moving, by the fact that my jeans were soaked, clinging to my legs. By my dull, myopic gaze. She didn't get out of the car, and I didn't go around to my side, to the driver's door. Instead, I opened her door and – this demonstrates the state I was in – went down on a knee beside her, resting my head against her body. To feel the warmth. That reassurance of her realness, of our existence. I didn't say anything to confirm it – nothing like, 'You were right' or 'It's him' – since it was self-evident. But I did say I had to call. She handed me my phone and, still kneeling, I held it up to check for signal. I had one flickering bar: just enough. I pressed nine three times and then slid my thumb to the dial button. But I didn't press it. I just stayed like that, penitent.

Mari said, 'Let me.'

I let her take the phone, but told her, 'I've got to do something, first.'

She looked at me, curious, as I laboured to my feet.

What I did next felt very natural to me, but must have looked strange to her. I opened the back door and got out the golf club, and the box of balls. Later, it would be hard to explain – to the emergency crew, to Deborah – but at the time it seemed the appropriate thing to do.

'OK,' I said to Mari. 'You better call them, now.'

As she did, I carried my burden away along shore, through the mist, to the place where the car had gone into the water. I slowly and deliberately stripped off the packing tape and removed the padded plastic wrapping from the golf club. It had a sleek rubber grip and a titanium head. It felt light and vibrant, reflecting the same soft sheen as the reservoir surface.

I tossed the wrapping aside and held up the club, like a staff. I felt like I ought to say something, to say a few words, but all I could come up with was, 'Well, Al – I guess it doesn't really matter either way.' And I'd never called him Al in my life.

Putting the club aside, I tore open the pack of balls. The box came with a few tees, and a ball marker for putting. I still have the marker, actually. Another keepsake secreted away in my drawers – the last from that time. I took one of the tees and stuck it in the mud and balanced a ball on it. Then I took up the driver again and adopted a golfing stance.

I'd never been much of a golfer and hadn't done any since the few times Alan and I had visited the driving range together. But now I felt the pressure to get it right – to hit the sweet spot. I took a few practice swings first, winding up a slow backswing, and uncoiling like a spring. The head of the driver made a satisfying whoosh.

I stepped forward. Lined up the club head with the ball and tee. I thought of my wife, back at the car, doing the right thing and making the call I hadn't been able to. I wanted to believe that it wouldn't always be like this, that I could be better, could become better. For her and for our child. And that I was different in some fundamental way to Alan. I wasn't sure, though. So I drew back the club and let swing. The head struck like a gong and I felt it resonate through my forearms. My first shot was low, so low that it actually skimmed across the water a few times, like a stone, before slipping beneath. I stooped and teed up another. I got the height on that one. The ball sailed out high and far, like a fishing lure, and landed with a satisfying splosh.

They weren't all like that. They went high and

low, landed near and far. Either way, the end result was always the same: a small splash, the echo and the ripple, and the surface re-establishing itself like a glaze. It made no difference, but I kept hitting them. I hit them until there were none left.

The Lion and the Star

Eluned Gramich

ELUNED GRAMICH was born in Haverfordwest and is a Welsh-German writer and translator. She won the People and Places: New Welsh Writing Award in 2015 with a memoir based on her experiences of Hokkaido, Japan, *Woman Who Brings the Rain*. She was also runner-up in the Terry Hetherington Award 2015 and short-listed for the Bristol Short Story Prize in 2011. Her writing has appeared in *New Welsh Short Stories*, *Stand*, *The Lonely Crowd*, *Rarebit*, *Wales Arts Review*, *New Welsh Review* and *Notes on the Underground*.

I fy rhieni

For my parents

CARDIGANSHIRE, 1972

KITES

IT'S EARLY AND Seren has been walking for hours. It's a long way from Cae Manon to the sea. Longer than she expected. On her journey, Seren passes one tractor, two Morris Minors, and Dai Trisant walking his collies. Old Dai raises his cap to her. She doesn't have a cap to raise, even though it's a cold morning in late March – with rain on the way. She doesn't have Pearl's blue mittens with her either, or the Afghan coat she borrowed from some long-ago friend who never asked for it back.

There. The sea. The afterglow of dawn still hanging in the sky. They say you can see Ireland from here on a clear day, but this is a lie. Seren has been living at Cae Manon camp for ten months. She's seen the mild summer and freezing winter, the badgers shambling across the road and the blue tits in the hedgerows, the ploughing and the tilling, the shearing and the lambing – but she's never seen Ireland. She has only ever seen Bardsey and the islets whose names she forgets.

Seren slips through the kissing gate and crosses the wide, wet field to the cliff edge. Her ankle-length skirt is drenched in dew; her feet are numb. The grass brushes against her calves as she weaves between the sheep droppings. Pearl once taught her about animal droppings. (It's the sort of thing Pearl liked to talk about.) She said that some animal droppings smelled worse than others. It goes: rabbit, sheep, cow, pig, dog, cat. Cat is the worst: if you touch it, the stink stays with you all day.

Today, strangely, there's no livestock to be seen. Only the pale grass and the Irish sea, which is grey and riven through with white foam. On her left is the TV mast, the tallest structure for miles. It stands with its arms extended upwards, a giant needle wrapped in iron wool and covered in satellite disks.

Once Seren has reached the far side, she peers over the edge. The waves crash against the cliff-face. They swell upwards, as if a watery fist is punching from the sea floor. It thrills her to see the waves break on the rocks, vanishing in an instant. She moves closer.

It starts to rain.

Seren has been walking for so long now, it feels strange to stop. She continues along the coast. The grass is thicker here, matted, slipping down the side of the cliff. If she carries on in this direction, she'll arrive at the village of Blaenplwyf. On the days that the three of them – Pearl, Jim and herself – hitch-hiked into town, they went through Blaenplwyf. The signs passed by: Blaenplwyf. Llanfarian. Rhydyfelin. Llanbadarn. Aberystwyth. Seren would say the names under her breath, practising the sounds. This would annoy Jim. Once, Pearl asked, 'How do you know the names?' And she replied, 'You only need to read the signs.'

There. A kite. Hovering. Searching for rabbits and moles. She's surprised to see it when the sky is so overcast and the rain is extending its fine net of drizzle over everything. The kite is poised above the ground, beak down, keeping its invisible spot in the air as if hanging from the sky by a string.

Barcud. The Welsh name comes to her then, echoing in her head. Kite. *Barcud. Gavião. Halcón. Habicht.* The more names come to her, the further she drifts away from the hovering bird. She thinks, instead, of the birds cruising across the fazendas, the Brazilian sun burning their wings; she thinks of the Yucatan nightjars in the Mexican forest, and the eagles in Arizona; she thinks of the red-tailed hawks in Maine and the fat buzzards in Scotland. And above these sky creatures, another hovers. An exceptional bird, holding the strings. A white bird, long-limbed. She tries to remember its name. It won't come to her now. All she has is *Barcud, Barcud, Barcud* echoing in her head.

She's come so close to the edge that the white of the sky has become the white of the foam. She's staring down the cliff-face. She thinks: Today it will really happen.

'Hey! Hey! Hey!'

She whips around, but there's no one else. She's alone. The slim line of beach below is empty. She looks up as though it was the bird calling her. But the kite has gone. The rain is too heavy for it.

'Heeeey!'

A tiny figure is waving at her from the top of the TV mast. At least, she thinks it's waving. It's difficult to make out its arms and legs through the low cloud. There is definitely something moving. The figure is shouting at her, but she can only hear Heeeh – Eeeee – Heeeeh – Eeee.

She glances at the waves one last time, then trudges over towards the mast. The figure is standing on the uppermost level, where the ladder stops. Seren shields her eyes from the rain and peers up at a young man. She immediately knows he should not be there. For starters, he's not wearing a hard hat or fluorescents. When he waves at her, he waves a flat cap like Dai Trisant's. Also, he seems to have tied himself to the platform. The biggest clue, however, is the banner hanging from the mast. On it are enormous letters, daubed in bright red ink. She takes a few steps back to mouth the words.

Ble mae'r Gymraeg?

Seren considers this for a moment, trying to decipher the question. (At least, she knows it must be a question.) Only, the words don't open themselves up to her or reveal their meaning. Frustration flashes through her: if she could understand these three words, she'd know why the man was standing on the mast, shouting at her. It might be something political, judging by the banner and the way he's tied himself to the metal frame. Didn't Jim mention protests once? But she's forgotten the reason for it now. Seren doesn't read the papers and news doesn't travel as far as their cabin in Cae Manon. There was that day when they couldn't get a ride to Aberystwyth because of demonstrations. She remembers Jim saying something about students blocking a bridge in town.

And there were bombs, too, apparently. Jim said they set them off in empty caravans.

She looks up at the man, but it's difficult to tell, at this distance, whether she's looking up at someone who plants bombs in caravans.

He motions for her to come nearer. At the bottom of the mast, she sees the evidence of his preparations: a drenched backpack, a bike propped up against a cement foundation block, a red sticker smacked against the electricity warnings. He's still shouting his head off, but she can only hear the Heeees and Aaaaahs.

She screams up at him: 'I don't understand you!'

His words fall on her with the rain: 'Pleeease! Taaaaake! Biiiiiiike!'

'What?'

'Biiiiiiiiike!'

'What?'

'Biiiiiiiiike!'

She picks up the bike and squints up at him. He seems to be waving his arms energetically in the direction of the road.

'Poh – liiiiiiiis!' he cries.

'What police?' she asks quite normally with no hope of being heard. She looks around but sees no one.

'Poh – liiiiis!' he screams over and over again, shaking his hat at the road. 'Poh – liiiiiiiis!'

'You want me to fetch the police here?' Her voice vanishes in the wind.

She takes a deep breath. Unfortunately, this man, whoever he is, doesn't know that he's picked the wrong person for the job. Seren is not a cyclist. In fact, she has never sat on a bike before. In Scotland, they had the van. In Maine, they had the bus. In Brazil, Vater had a car and a truck. And before that? She doesn't remember what she had before that.

Seren pushes the mud-splattered bike to the road and examines it for a moment. She locates the pedals; spins the front wheel. She swings a leg over experimentally and perches on the saddle. It's heavier than it looks. The colour is a rusted brown, the seat surprisingly low. Taped to the handlebars is a fifty-pence coin. Apart from that, there aren't any instructions. She regards the road ahead: single-lane. The hedgerows are high on both sides, making it impossible to see what might be hurtling towards her. The road dips and rises with the coast before plunging into the village.

'What are you doing up there anyway?' she mutters. Lucky I came along, she thinks. What would you have done without me?

He waves at her with both hands: a crazy, desperate semaphore. Maybe he really has lost his mind. What does he want now?

When she squints, she realises he's giving her the thumbs up and cheering her on.

TELEPHONE

SHE WALKS THE bike along with her feet like a child. Blushing, knowing that the man is watching her from the mast. He must think she's daft. Still, she goes careful, pushes on little by little, lifts her feet, puts them on the ground, lifts them up again. Tip-toeing down the road, feeling her way forward...

Until something strange happens: her body cycles for her.

That is: she's thinking about one thing – calling the police, not letting down the stranger who's cheering her from the top of the TV mast – yet her body is doing something else entirely. Her feet have placed themselves on the pedals. They're going round and round, turning the wheels like an ordinary, unselfconscious person. The sort of competent person who can ride bikes and doesn't live in a cabin off-grid. There's no swerving, not even a pre-emptory wobble. Her body pitches forward to accelerate, and backwards when it squeezes the brakes, as if it was all completely natural.

Seren thinks: All this time I thought I couldn't ride a bike, and now it turns out I was born to do it.

Her flowing skirt catches in the spokes. She stops, rolls it up and tucks it in her waistband. Beneath her skirt she wears a pair of scarlet leg warmers Pearl knitted for her when they arrived in Skye the year before last. The leg warmers aren't much use in a downpour. They're sagging with rain. She has to stop again to take them off, shoving them into the pocket of her cardigan. She hopes they're not spoiled. Pearl only knits for Seren and herself (Jim being critical of bright colours).

Wait until I tell them about this, she thinks. They won't believe me at first. But I'll show them. I'll show them I'm a useful person who can ride bikes.

There's a sharp curve to navigate before she gets to Blaenplwyf. She handles it expertly, knee out, swinging into the road. Fearless. She arrives with her legs bare and pink with cold; her rosy underwear has turned a dark red.

The main street is quiet; the newsagent doors are closed and there's no light in the window. Perhaps the bad weather has frightened them off. A ginger cat sits under the porch of one of the Victorian grey-stone houses, curling his tail languidly in the air.

Seren swiftly dismounts. Her body knows what must be done. She puts her weight on one foot while lifting the other cleanly over the bar. She props the bike against the phone box and unwraps the fifty-pence coin.

Fifty pence will get her a lengthy conversation with the police, which Seren doesn't want. None of her previous conversations with the police have gone in her favour. The police like to have papers, details, addresses. It's exhausting having to explain her life in a way an official can understand. They might as well be asking the question **BLE MAE'R GYMRAEG?** over and over.

Perhaps it will be all right this time. They'll be too distracted with the man on the mast to care about her and she'll be free to go . . .

But where will she go?

It doesn't matter about that now, she thinks. She has a job to do. She flicks through the grubby phonebook stuffed under the telephone and dials the number.

'Good morning. You've reached Aberystwyth Police Station. How may I be of assistance?'

'Hello,' she says. And sighs. It's that familiar tone again: clipped and confident. Policemen around the world have it.

'This is Constable Davies. To whom am I speaking?'

The word echoes in her mind: Constable. *Constable.* Ironically, it's very close to the word Comfortable. Come for table. Con. Stable. A stable for horses, or a stable foundation. A con for stealing money, or con as in the Spanish word for *with*.

'He-llo?'

'I'm calling because there's a man stuck up the TV mast.'

'Llew Roberts, is it?'

'I don't know.'

'He's gone up Blaenplwyf?'

'There's a man up the TV mast. I don't know if it's the man you think it is.'

'Stupid bugger. How long has he been up there for?'

'I don't know.'

'You calling from the phone box in the village, is it?'

'Yes.'

'He's not coming down, do you think? Wait. Let

128

me say that again. Does he look like he wants to come down?'

Seren remembers the cord the man used to tie himself to the mast. 'Not really.'

'Tell him the sergeant is on his way.'

'All right.'

'Who are you then? I don't recognise your voice.'

'Seren,' she says.

'Ti'n siarad cymraeg, te?'

'What?'

'Fine, Seren. On our way, tell him.'

She puts the phone down. The tabby is stretching across the porch step, paws pointing towards her, claws out. Seren goes and sits next to it, murmurs, 'Hello, boy. Hello, you ginger terror, have you caught any mice today?' The cat flops on its back and offers up its stomach for rubbing. 'I bet you can eat a lot of mice, can't you? A big boy like you.'

Seren's skirt is still tucked into her waistband. She doesn't bother unrolling it as she'll only have to roll it up again. The cat's soft paws hang in the air; it starts to purr.

She'll have to take the bike back to him, this man who might be Llew Roberts. She doesn't want to wait for the police, but perhaps she'll have to – otherwise they might go looking for her . . . She doesn't like this idea: she's had enough people looking for her in the past. People who wanted to do her harm.

Would Jim be looking for her now? Would Pearl? She hopes they are, but it's difficult to say for certain.

It still feels early. There's no one moving behind the windows; no one tinkering with the car or painting the windowpanes. She imagines Jim and Pearl lying next to each other in the cabin, wrapped up in the quilts and sheep-skin covers they'd brought down from the community on Skye, and spread on top of it all, the Afghan coat.

She should have brought the coat with her. Only, she didn't think she'd be needing it. At least, a part of her was sure that she wouldn't be needing it. The other part of her hoped to see Pearl and Jim running across the field, calling her name.

She picks up the bike, swings her leg over the bar, and lets her body take over again.

AN INTERVIEW

THE POLICE ARE already there. Two of them.
They've parked the car haphazardly in the field. The
tyres have left deep muddy gouges. The younger of
the two (skinny, blond, sores on his chin) is about to
close the gate when she appears, legs still bare, water
dripping down her calves.

His lip curls when he sees her; she can't tell if he's
smiling or snarling.

'What are you doing here?' he asks.

'Let her in,' says the older policeman (forty-five,
broad shoulders, a real handlebar moustache). 'You
were the one who called in. I'm Sergeant Jones.'

She nods. The skinny officer opens the gate while
staring openly at her thighs.

'What do we have here then?' asks the moustached
sergeant, craning up at the mast.

'It's Llew Roberts, Sir.'

'I can see that, boy.'

Llew Roberts has stopped waving. In fact, he's sitting down, legs swinging between the bars. The banner still flaps in the wind, shouting: **BLE MAE'R GYMRAEG?**

'What's the plan, Sir?'

'Take your notebook out, boy. Do something useful.'

The boy does as he's told. His notebook is black, his pencil mechanical. He turns to her, demands her name, address, age, and she remembers why she hates policemen.

'*Excuse me*,' he's saying to her. 'Are you deaf or what?'

Sergeant Jones is climbing up the giant needle. There he goes, torso wider than the ladder, taking it two rungs at a time. Llew Roberts doesn't react: he's still swinging his legs from side to side quite cheerfully, as if this was exactly what he'd been hoping for. Boy gives up asking her questions and they stare, silently, as the sergeant heaves himself up towards the sky.

When he gets really high, so high that they have to twist their heads right back to see him, Boy lets out a low whistle.

'*Jesus* Christ,' he says.

The rain's coming down in sheets and the banner is flapping more wildly. But the sergeant pushes on, one hand on his helmet to stop it from flying off.

'They won't believe this down at the station,' says Boy, gawping.

She wants to tell him: if an angel were to pass by and blow on your face, you'd be stuck like that for ever. That's what they used to say on the ranch in Rio Branco when she was a girl. They believed in angels there, and spirits and all that stuff she is very slowly learning to un-believe. (Or believe differently. It's difficult to say.)

'Did you know about this?' Boy asks.

She shakes her head.

'Are you a girlfriend of Llew's then?'

She shakes her head again.

'I hear he's got a lot of girls, does Llew.'

The very tip of the mast is hidden in cloud, as if it's got stuck in the sky. If the clouds were any lower, the two figures would vanish completely, and then there would be nothing she could do except wait beside this policeman with terrible skin and hope . . . The idea of Llew Roberts vanishing fills her with dread.

Boy is staring at her. He's been staring at her for a

minute or so and she's been doing her best to ignore it.

'I've seen you around. You hang out with those hippies by Devil's Bridge.'

His tone is peculiar, as if deciding whether to charm or insult her. It quickly becomes clear which route he'll take.

'One of them's English, the bloke. The girl's American. I've heard her talk down in the market. Loud as fuck. But you. We've got bets on you. You're not from here, but you're not English either. So what are you?'

As Boy inches closer, his voice quietens. She wishes for something to distract him; she wishes Sergeant Jones would trip, or that Llew would start hurling stones. Anything to stop him from talking.

'In my experience, people who don't answer questions have something to hide.'

She wonders why Boy, the younger and more athletic of the two, is the one waiting at the bottom while his overweight boss is clambering up to the top.

'We think you're all nutters down at the station. Camping in the snow over the winter.'

'We don't camp,' she says. 'We have wooden cabins.'

'My *apologies*,' says Boy. She can feel his eyes on her, appraising her tanned skin and chestnut hair, before moving down across her chest, waist, to her thighs again.

She keeps her gaze fixed on Sergeant Jones' backside as it lifts up into the mist.

'Do you all do it with each other then? Free love and all that. Oh come on, you can tell me. There's no one else listening. Is it true you can just hop into bed with anyone you want?'

'Don't be stupid,' she says.

'I'd watch your language if I were you. Insulting a police officer is an offence.'

Her nails – sharp and black with soil – cut into the flesh of her palm.

'There's three of you. I've seen the bloke. Not much to look at, but he must be something if he keeps two women happy. What's his secret then? Does he have a huge dick, is that it?'

She walks away, but he follows her, grabs her arm. She flinches, and pulls away.

'Calm down, love. I'm only showing some healthy curiosity. It's not the end of the fucking world.'

At last, Sergeant Jones reaches the narrow circular platform. He sits down beside Llew. Now there are four legs, swinging in the air. He seems strangely happy to be up there, if the cheerful way the two embrace and slap each other on the back is anything to go by. The sergeant shields his eyes, taking in the view, while Llew points at the horizon.

'How will he get him down?' she asks herself.

'Oh, he'll come down now. He's just waiting to be arrested, the prick.'

The boy policeman is right. After a few moments' recovery, the sergeant gets to his feet and so does Llew. Sergeant Jones lets him go first, and the two men descend, like ants crawling down a tree trunk.

When they reach the ground, the sweating constable grins and says: 'Now there's a good story for the lads.'

Seren looks out of the foggy car window. The rain has, in Sergeant Jones' words, 'gone beyond'. It hammers down on the roof, drowning out the sound of conversation. She can hardly see anything of her early morning walk: the sea is obscured by fat raindrops.

How did she get here again?

This is her life: she heads in one direction and then she's taken in another against her will. She has such longings – longing to be outside, longing for

Cae Manon and Pearl, longing for those wide empty spaces where a person can simply drop off the map's edge ... All those longings have brought her to a police car outside Blaenplwyf.

'Name?'

Boy has been asking this for some time now. He's sitting next to her in the back. Llew and the sergeant are up front. They haven't bothered with the handcuffs. They haven't even locked the doors or put the key in the ignition. Llew is directly in front of her: the most she can see is his wild hair, dark and curly with rain. The sergeant and Llew are conducting their own 'interview' in the front: it doesn't sound like any interview she's had. Their voices are loud and boisterous. From time to time, they burst into laughter.

'She's not answering my questions,' Boy interrupts, sounding bitter.

'She doesn't have to answer them. She hasn't done anything wrong,' says Llew.

The sergeant catches her eye in the rear-view mirror. 'You told me your name was Seren.'

She nods.

'Are you from Wales, then, with a name like that?'

She shakes her head.

Boy pipes up: 'She doesn't look Welsh. Or English either. Looks a bit Spanish, if anything.'

'Well, *bach*, are you Spanish?'

She just smiles at that.

The sergeant tries again: 'What's your surname?'

'Gold,' she says.

'Seren Gold? Pull the other one. How old are you?'

'Twenty-nine.'

Boy curses under his breath.

'Twenty-nine. *Duw*, you don't look twenty-nine.' The sergeant starts the engine. 'Off we go!' he says, before pulling out into the road.

She presses her face against the window, stares up at the TV mast where the banner is still fluttering in the wind. Strange, she thinks. Why hasn't the sergeant pulled it down?

They're about to turn the corner when Llew cries, 'Wait! What about my bike?'

Sergeant Jones slams the brakes.

Boy shouts in alarm: 'Forget your fucking bike, man!'

'Now, now,' says the Sergeant. 'What do you want to do, Llew? Stick it under the hedge over there until you get back?'

Llew turns in his seat so that he's half-kneeling, facing her.

'Seren. Listen. I know we don't know each other and I know I'm asking a lot from you. But, see, the bike is my favourite thing in the world. It belongs to my dad. He'd kill me if he came out and heard that I'd left it up here to rust. Could you take it down to my Mamgu for me? She lives in Trefechan, the house with the pond. Lan y Môr it's called. Do you know Trefechan? Oh *Duw*. Well. How about this then – take it to the Coops. Ask to see Eurig. He works the day shift. Tell him what happened – it'll cheer him up.'

Seren looks in his eyes, which are grey with spots of green, and says, 'All right then.'

COOPER'S ARMS

THE PUB STICKS out into the crossroad like an elbow on a crowded bus. Everything about the Coops is close to the ground – the door is low, the windows crooked and squashed like an Elizabethan facade. Steps lead down from the street into the dim, smoky rooms. The word *Tafarn* floats into her head. It drags behind it the other words she has used once: pub, inn, *el bar*, *boteco*, *kneipe*. And behind those, there is another word still, glittering in the dark like a gold coin in a copper fountain.

'Jesus. Did you swim here?'

A knot of people are conversing in low tones on the far side of the pub, underneath the earthenware jugs and silver horseshoes. A few retirees sit at the counter. Seren is surprised: it's not yet noon and the place is almost full. The barman leans over the taps, looking up at her where she's still standing on the steps.

'Hey! I asked you a question. Did you swim here, *bach*?'

'Sorry?'

'You're soaked through.'

'Oh.'

'Aren't you freezing cold?'

She quickly untucks her skirt, colouring. But no, she isn't cold. In fact, it's sweltering in the pub. There's condensation on the walls, her fingertips gather it as she walks to the bar. The room is thick with cigarette smoke. She inhales it, enjoying the woozy effect it has on her, that momentary forgetfulness. She also inhales the odour of cider and malt, of course, and another smell, like burnt meat.

The barman is everything she imagines a barman should be: big, wide as a barrel, his dark-brown beard flecked with white. His corduroy shirt is open, revealing tufts of grey hair. She doesn't want to speak to him – she doesn't feel like speaking to anybody after the police car – but he's expecting something from her. They all are. She is being stared at. The barman's eyes are directed downwards, where her skirt sticks to her legs. A glance here and there from the two men at the counter and the knot of young people (Are they students? How she wishes she were a student). There's a lull in conversation, more curious than hostile. Seren is acutely aware of the way her cardigan clings to her breasts.

'Are you Eurig?' she asks the barman.

'I am. Who's asking?'

'I've got Liu's bike.'

'Who?'

A retiree looks up from his pint: 'She means Llew.'

Eurig straightens up. 'My God. You've seen him? Where's he now?'

'I don't know.'

The customer looks down at his beer again.

'I think they arrested him,' she says.

The knot springs apart. The students rush to the bar, pints in hand, until Seren finds herself surrounded by people all talking at once.

'Did he do it?'

'Is he all right?'

'Did they get him?'

'Are you sure it was him?'

'Is this some hippy joke you're playing?'

'Did he do it, really now?'

She instinctively turns towards the exit, but there

are people there, blocking her way. Questions, more questions. She leans over the bar, trying to hide herself. A water drop rolls down her nose and falls into someone's drink.

'Well?' they say. 'Did he do it?'

'Yes,' she says slowly. 'But I don't know why.'

The presence of these strangers is almost like being blinded. She can't see properly when there are so many people she doesn't know; her mind is working too hard, thinking too much. It can't perform its normal functions. They're so young. Twenty, twenty-one. Eight years younger than Seren. Curious girls and boys, pressing close, as if desperate for distraction. They're speaking Welsh; although she can recognise the language, she can't follow it. She only knows the words Dai Trisant taught her for cow, sheep, dog, cat, pig and bird. The word for slow and road and thank you. Also, she knows what her own name means, because you would have to be a very stupid person to not know the meaning of the name you chose for yourself.

The young people want a story. They ask her for it. She tries to explain, but she's afraid she's telling it wrong. The wrong bits in the wrong order. Their expressions are full of impatience, waiting for a punchline she isn't delivering.

'He was just up there waving at me and I got the bike and I rode down to the telephone box to call the police and they came and then one of them climbed up and then they both climbed down and then they drove him away, but before he went he told me to come here with the bike. Or he told me to take the bike to Lanymor.'

'Lan y Môr. That's his family home, see,' says Eurig. But none of the others are interested in Llew's family home.

'Where was he? How did he get up?'

'How did he come down?'

'Could you read the banner from a distance? Was it clear?'

Eurig leans in conspiratorially, tells her: 'They threw his parents in prison.'

'Oh,' is all she says, because now everyone is talking very fast in Welsh again. She wishes she could leave but knows she can't. Not yet. She's part of their excitement, their newly discovered joy, and they want more. More details. More information. Even though she was there, she finds herself struggling to remember. Her answers are not satisfactory.

How did he seem when he got down? Sad? Hurt? Triumphant? She says, I don't know.

What did the police say, are they going to charge him? She says, I don't know.

Some of the students are wearing red stickers like the one Llew had stuck on the mast.

Eurig cuts across them, waves his arms: 'Woah, hold on now. All these questions and not one of you stingy bastards has offered the girl a drink. What will you have? A shandy?'

She looks up at this, smiles for the first time. 'Guinness, please.'

'You sure? We do a good shandy. Put it in a lady's glass for you and all.'

'No, thank you. Pint of Guinness please.'

Eurig grins. 'Wouldn't have put you down for a beer drinker.'

She doesn't know what to say to that. Is she too small for a pint of stout, too weak? He doesn't know anything about her: he doesn't know what she's capable of. Smallness has nothing to do with strength. Has he never watched a boxing match? Lightweight or middleweight or heavyweight – what does it matter? You can still knock a man down, whatever your size.

'Here, *bach*. A glass of what's good for you.'

She's grateful for the Guinness; she can tell the story better now. She describes the two policemen (they know, it seems, who she means), and how Sergeant Jones sat down with Llew, legs dangling in the air (they like that and whoop with laughter).

'I can't imagine Jones climbing all that way. He gets winded going up Constitution Hill.'

'Reckon he'll let Llew off?'

'They might keep him in overnight.'

'Has anyone phoned the papers yet?'

The Guinness calms and warms her while the students continue their chatter. She can feel Eurig watching her, perched on the stool, both hands on the pint glass, drinking the stout down.

'You want something with that? Packet of crisps?'

'No, thank you.'

She knows she should be on her way, but she can't help herself. Anyway, there is nowhere for her to go.

A blonde-haired girl lights a cigarette, inhales and bursts into a fit of coughing.

'Give it here,' says Seren, and plucks it from her fingers.

The girl's eyes are watering.

'I have questions too,' Seren says. 'Everyone's

147

asking *me* what happened. *Me*. The person who knows the least.'

'I wouldn't say that,' says Eurig.

'I don't even know how to say his name.'

He laughs. 'What do you want to know?'

'What did the banner say?' she asks. She'd been too embarrassed to admit in front of the students that she hadn't understood; wanted to pretend, for some reason, that she knew Llew, knew his convictions and motivations.

Eurig puts the glasses back on the shelf behind him, still dripping water from the plunger. 'I don't know. I didn't see it, *bach*.'

'Why was he up there in the first place?'

'He did it for the television channel.'

What? She raises her hand, swatting his words away. She doesn't like this reason. She was hoping for something more ... more romantic. Something that would make sense to her.

'What television channel?'

'The Welsh one we were promised. The Tories lied. Said we'd be getting our own programmes in our own language. As soon as they got into Number 10, they changed their minds.'

'I don't watch television,' she says.

'I imagine there's not much electricity up there by Devil's Bridge.'

'No,' she concedes. 'We have a power generator. It runs for a maximum of two hours before it overheats. There's a risk of explosion. When it overheats, I mean.'

Eurig shakes his head.

There's only two inches of Guinness left. She tips the murky liquid left and right. A sad state of affairs. The barman sighs, starts on the next pint while giving her a funny kind of smile as if to say, this is all you're getting. If she had been a man he'd have pulled her another without hesitation. She likes to drink. So what? At Cae Manon, she wasn't allowed. Pearl wouldn't allow it. She knitted her clothes and made the quilts for her bed and told her never to drink again.

'You can leave the bike round the back once you've finished,' he says, putting the pint down in front of her. It's mostly head. He's rushed it; he wants her gone.

'Where does Liu live?'

'Over the bridge towards Pen Dinas. Then up on the right . . .'

The old man at the counter looks up perfunctorily, says, 'The posh bit,' before looking down again.

The barman adds: 'His mamgu thinks she's something better. Her husband went to Oxford and spoke eleven languages.'

A gust of cold air causes her to turn round. Someone is grappling with the door, trying to pull it open against the wind and rain that's picked up outside. She tenses up as a pair of muddy brown boots appear on the steps. She mutters: 'Jim.'

He comes into the pub and the crowd that has gathered around Seren immediately disperses. How do they know to do that? Can they sense what is about to happen, or is it Jim himself – the way his hair almost reaches his elbow, his smell of damp and woodsmoke and weed – that compels them to back away?

Jim takes her arm and steers her towards the window. 'You crazy bitch. You can't just take off like that.'

Take auhph, he says, all New York. But Jim is not from America; he was born in Colchester, but left his parents to go and live on Long Island and never went back.

His face is very close to hers; he doesn't have

enough beard to hide his hollow cheeks. The hollowness makes his teeth look enormous. How did she ever think he was handsome?

'Let me go.'

'I'm sorry.' He drops her wrist. 'I shouldn't have said that. I shouldn't have said crazy bitch. We were worried. We went to the police. They told us you'd be here.' He looks around the room, as if realising where he is. 'Why *are* you here? Are you drinking again?'

'I'm here because you kicked me out,' she says. 'You want to go find your *roots* in fucking Ireland without me.'

He tucks his bottom lip under his large front teeth. It's strange how different you feel after only a few hours, she thinks. Eight or nine hours earlier and she thought she was in love. And now she can't even speak to him in the way she used to: that eager, pleasing way of the day before. The weeks and months before.

'Stupid girl. You know we didn't want you to go straight away. Not like this, not at dawn in the pouring rain. No money, no coat, not even a fucking goodbye. We want you to stay until you get yourself another place. Make sure you're settled. Didn't I say that? Didn't I make that clear?'

'Where is she?'

She has her answer as soon as she asks the question. Through the squat, grimy window, she sees her. Pearl. Opposite the pub under an umbrella, waiting for him and hiding from her. Pearl's mane of blue-blonde hair is tied up in a bun and she is not smiling.

'You know this is very hard for her,' says Jim.

Although you wouldn't say that if you looked at her now, Seren thinks, standing very straight in the Afghan coat, staring at the pub with a determined, almost defiant expression.

Seren starts talking. It's the beer. She surprises herself: 'Something changed, Jim, and I don't know what it is. I've been trying to think about what it is *exactly*. But I've realised that there's no point wasting any more time on something I'll probably never understand.'

'It's not just one thing, Seren. It's a combination of factors. It's the whole situation. This place. Our Cae Manon. The atmosphere we create together at a given moment. The vibrations in us that we can't control. We're not always the same people, if you see what I mean. We're not the same as we were in Skye or when we met in the forest in Pine Knoll, you remember? We're changing, always changing, like the air is changing, like the seasons change.'

'Shut up.'

Jim purses his bloodless lips. '*Fine*. If you want to be like that, fine. It's you. It's all you. *Your* behaviour.'

Seren wonders if Pearl is cold out there in the rain. She has such pale skin, like milk.

'You cry when you sleep, did you know that? Do you remember the night you howled outside the cabin for hours?'

'Stop making things up.'

'We can't ignore it any more. It upsets Pearl.'

Seren knew Pearl before Jim. For about one hour and twenty-five minutes – the time it took to hitch-hike from the station to the camp in Pine Knoll. Pearl put her arm around her and said: 'Do you see that snowy ridge over there? Where the rooks are? That's Canada.' Then, it had been Pearl and Seren. Always together. But she was not called Seren back then. She still had the name her adopted mother had given her. And before this name there'd been another name.

But she shouldn't think about that now.

Seren puts her hand in her cardigan pocket. It's soaking wet. Jim has returned to the subject of inter-personal vibrations. These vibrations, he says, have waned. The atmosphere has turned sour. What they had together has (temporarily?) vanished, in the same way that sound vibrations vanish after the music has finished playing. They need to go to Ireland without her; *he* needs to go without her. They can't carry on as they are. Later, once he has found his ancestral home in Galway (she laughs at this – Ancestral!), the way forward might be clearer. He's sorry he called her a crazy bitch. He called her a crazy bitch because he loves her and was afraid she'd done something she shouldn't have.

'You talk too much,' she says, pushing past him to the door.

She crosses the road without looking. Pearl recoils, glances right and left as if she's about to be attacked. But it's me, only me, Seren thinks. Your quiet brown mouse. Why is Pearl looking at her like that? Why is she drawing the coat so tightly across her body?

'I know this is you,' Seren says.

'I don't know what you mean.'

'You're behind this. Jim would never ask me to leave without your say-so.'

For all Jim's talk of vibrations, of wrong and right times, of wavelengths and not feeling each other and the rest, Seren knows the real reason she has been asked to leave. The reason is so disappointing it hurts.

'You're jealous. I know you are. You think I'll take Jim away from you, but I won't. I won't. We were happy as a three. I was happy as the third. That's all I ever wanted. I want things to stay – to stay as they are.' Suddenly, it's difficult to speak, because she realises that things are about to change, are changing, all over again.

Pearl isn't listening. Her voice is unusual, quiet. 'Why did you walk off like that without saying any-thing?'

'Why did you ask Jim to talk to me? Why didn't you do it yourself?'

'We went to the police. Did Jim say? I was so frightened. You're always frightening me.'

'I want my coat back.'

'It's not your coat.'

Seren takes the ball of sodden wool from her pocket and throws it at her. It smacks Pearl right in the chest, sticking to her suede lapel like a lump of red gore, before dropping to the ground. 'Here. Your fucking leg warmers.'

Then something happens that takes her by surprise. Someone grabs hold of her hand and shoves it up her back. Seren screams and instantly sinks to the tarmac while Pearl cries, 'Stop it! Stop it!'

Jim loosens his hold. 'You crazy bitch!' he's saying. 'Don't fucking touch her!'

Seren pulls herself free and sprints across the road. 'I hate you! I hate you!'

She mounts the bike and is gone.

LAN Y MÔR

IT'S NOT MUCH of a bridge: a narrow, stone hump over the little estuary that flows into the marina. The tide is high, the water a swirling brown underneath. A small bridge like this is vulnerable – easy to blockade, easy to cut off. It was here that the protests happened; the ones that cut Cae Manon off from the town. Jim saw them, hundreds of students, sitting on the concrete in their coats and scarves, and red-painted signs. It is the only bridge into town from the north; the town shrank in a matter of hours, the markets cancelled, the hospital closed. Two police officers are guarding it on either side. Afraid, perhaps, that the students might file out of the pub and decide to cut off the town again.

In the marina are fishing boats and leisure boats and little dinghies. The ropes on the empty flag posts flutter in the wind, making a strange ringing sound.

The police officers observe her in silence. On the bike, she is unstoppable.

A sign. She mouths the word: *Trefechan*. She has good pronunciation. Dai Trisant told her so. She can roll her 'r's like no one else.

Of course she's heard of the area. Trefechan is the well-off part of town; Jim (ugly, foul, traitorous Jim) said it was a den of bourgeoisie. All detached bungalows and pruned front lawns. She's heard people talk of the countryside behind it, too, the hilltop called Pen Dinas on which the Victorians built a brick pillar for reasons only Victorians could understand and where the Stone Age people lived in their round houses.

Her shoulder aches from where Jim grabbed her. But gradually, as she glides through the streets, she forgets the pain. She passes garden after garden, house after house: shipshape family homes with their own names nailed to the walls. *Bodnant. Arianrhod. Llygad yr Haul.* The houses get further and further apart, until the street narrows and becomes little more than a potholed path. At the end of it stands a square, stone-walled building, its lower half concealed by perennials and creepers, the top dominated by a thin-looking bay window. There are two chimneys sending out billowing white smoke.

In the mess of the front garden – a jungle of grass, bushes and knotted undergrowth – she spots a pool of black water.

She pushes the bike up towards the house, gazing all the time at the water, afraid that something might emerge from the depths. Dispersed across the garden are little clues to its upkeep. Shining, metallic globes stick out of the ground, and there are gnomes too – a goblin with red hair and a yellow shirt, grinning at the murky pond, as if he too suspects there is something living in it.

Seren pauses on the garden path for a long while. The cold has finally caught up with her. It has settled inside her and she's shivering as she grips the handlebars. There are many questions running through her mind and she doesn't have an answer for any of them. These include:

Should she leave the bike here?

Should she go to the door and explain about the mast and the police?

If she leaves the bike here, where will she go?

Should she go to Cae Manon and get her coat?

Or beg them to take her back?

Will Pearl still look after her if she asks kindly?

If she says she loves her, her only sister, friend?

Is it really over?

Should she go back to the cliffs?

There's no straightforward answer to any of these questions. She doesn't even know where to leave the bike. Her fingers are red and raw from the cold. The shivering worsens.

She hears shouting.

'Don't touch a single leaf!'

A corpse is leaning out of the bay window. It has a shock of white hair like a halo and speaks with the deepest voice she has ever heard. A long black sleeve trails over the sill.

'Don't touch anything. He planted hemlock and I can't say for certain where it is.'

Seren glances at the garden, then up again.

'We had an incident with a cat recently,' the corpse says. 'What are you standing there for? Bring it round the back. But don't touch anything there either.'

The window shuts.

The back of the house is not much different from the front, apart from a forlorn shed and a wicker chair, brown with mould. She leans the bike against the wall, taking care not to disturb the dead-looking pot plants. The back door opens.

'Leave it there. He can deal with it when he's back.'

She feels guilty for having thought the woman was a corpse. She's done her hair up now; her skin is still ashen, paler even than Pearl, but taken all together the corpse is a human woman after all. In fact, Seren even finds that she's somewhat beautiful. Striking anyway, in her fine, black clothes – a buttoned-up jacket with conical sleeves, a woollen skirt straight as a baton.

'I'm Llew's grandmother. Myfanwy Roberts.'

'Seren Gold.'

The woman looks her up and down. 'You'd better come inside.'

She opens the door and, a moment later, Seren finds herself in Mrs Roberts' front room, standing as close to the fire as possible, her hands almost touching the metal screen.

'I'll get you a change of clothes. Although any of mine will be far too small for you. You can fit Llew's shirts, I dare say. Warm yourself up a bit while I get them.'

Seren would have perched on the tweed-covered

footstool given the choice, but Mrs Roberts won't hear of it. She leads her back from the fire a little, sits her down on the dark green sofa. The floorboards creak overhead. The room smells of wood burning and ink. Seren sits very still, not wanting to be accused of something (breakages, theft, impropriety). She feels rather than sees the presence of valuable objects: books and pictures and trinkets; shawls and carpets and candlesticks.

She gazes into the fire and thinks, when have I been here before? Because she is sure she has been here before. If not this room exactly, then another very like it. A library, perhaps, in São Paulo. Or the apartment of the teacher she'd briefly lived with in Maine. Or perhaps she's just reminded of photographs in magazines, or television interviews with famous authors, performed in front of walls of books ...

Mrs Roberts returns, carrying a folded flannel shirt patterned with mauve and blue squares, a pair of corduroys, thick socks and a peach-coloured towel.

'Might as well get changed by the fire,' she tells Seren. 'Upstairs is as cold as ice.'

Mrs Roberts ducks under an arch that leads to a

small kitchen. An iron kettle is blowing steam on the stove, a teapot standing by.

'Just boiled. I was expecting you.'

Seren takes off her wet things until she's completely naked in Mrs Roberts' front room. She rubs herself down with the peach towel before stepping into Llew's clothes. They fit as if they were made for her.

'Are you decent?'

A strange question, she thinks.

'Yes.'

'Warm?'

'Yes.'

Mrs Roberts stands in the archway. Even though she is far smaller than Seren, it feels as though she is looking down at her.

'The children will be pleased,' she says.

'Does he have children?'

'Fifty-six to be precise. At Llanbadarn School. He teaches French and German there. He hadn't told them of his plans, of course, but they'll be happy when they hear of it, I'm sure. Quite the story for the classroom. Perhaps they'll even think of studying Welsh later on in life after having such a heroic teacher. But most of those girls and boys these days want to be astronauts. Or athletes. Or actors. All things beginning with "a" it seems. As if they can't go any further down the alphabet. Such limited imaginations these days. It's quite awful really.'

'You think a child who wants to be an astronaut has a limited imagination?'

'Of course. People are so fixated on finding out more about the most absurd things. Space! Everyone wants to know about planets and stars and orbits. I'm sure it's all very interesting. But why not study something closer to home? Languages, for instance. People are rushing off investigating sharks, and orangutans, and asteroids, and Amazon rainforests, and goodness knows what else, but they neglect the one truly miraculous ability we all share: the power of speech. Don't you agree?'

'I wouldn't know.'

'My late husband was a philologist. Cambridge. Anglo-Saxon, Norse and Celtic.'

'Oh.'

'It's why he married me. For my Welsh. And Breton, Irish Gaelic and Cornish. You'll always have something to talk about if you're interested in languages, because there's always more to learn.'

'Yes.'

'Will you have a biscuit? They were made by someone far more talented at baking than I.'

Seren takes one and holds it to her lips. No, it's no good. No appetite at all. The thought of eating makes her feel sick.

'I heard his parents were in prison?'

Mrs Roberts laughs. 'In prison! Yes, indeed they are.'

'I was wondering, why exactly...'

'Why indeed!' She laughs louder. 'Not paying their taxes.'

'Taxes?'

'That's right. Not paying their taxes and then, what was it? Refusing to attend trial.'

'How long will they be in prison for?'

'Six months. They'll be out in three with any luck.' She brushes the crumbs from her knee. 'They won't stay out long though. In a few weeks they'll be back again.'

'Oh. Do they have money troubles?'

'Goodness, no. I should think they have the expected amount of money trouble. They'll pay their taxes and respond to summons as soon as *they* send their correspondence in Welsh.'

'Oh,' says Seren. Then, because she is thankful for

the tea and the clothes and embarrassed that she can offer nothing in return, adds: 'I want to learn.'

'So you should.'

'I'd always thought I'd stay here for a while.' She pushes her friends from her mind: Jim's voice, so certain and assured, and Pearl's shocked expression on the street outside the Cooper's Arms. She doesn't want to think about that now.

A clock chimes the hour, a light, silvery sound. It makes her wince; she dislikes mechanical noises, bells and clockwork.

'You don't sound Welsh,' Seren says.

'Oh, but I am.' The tongs clatter on the table. Mrs Roberts pours the tea into two rose-petalled cups. 'Father was English, Mam was from Llanuwchllyn. Father sent me to private schools on the continent. This was before the war. Switzerland. Then southern Germany. Catholic boarding schools,' she says. 'I can't say I enjoyed it much at the time, but I've come to regard those years as an interesting interlude in my life. Something to draw on, you know, *creatively*. I think of those schools often, I admit. Nunneries in the Alps; fortresses of religion that hadn't changed in centuries. I wonder if they've changed now.'

Despite the heat from the fire, Seren is still

shivering. The cup trembles in her hands. She drinks quickly, burning her tongue.

'I spoke Welsh from birth, learned English from my father, German from my school fellows, French from my teachers. But it's Welsh that I returned to and live with now. Accents can be misleading, don't you agree? Yours, for instance . . .'

Seren thrusts her cup at her host. 'Is there any more, please?'

Mrs Roberts purses her lips. Perhaps she's not used to being interrupted. She pours the tea again before settling back on the armchair, her black-heeled feet on the footstool.

The fire spits; this means the wood is wet. Beneath the balls of newspaper and twigs, the coals are not yet red-hot. The shivering gets worse; Seren holds the cup with both hands, but the liquid slops onto Llew's shirt.

'I'm sorry, so sorry . . .'

Mrs Roberts gets up and retrieves from behind her chair a coffee table, stained with ink. She takes the cup from Seren's hands. Her white hair is not pinned, she sees, but done up in a French plait. The hair is so white and straw-like that it is difficult to make out the weave. Plait is another problematic word; a word

167

that dances around her mind with its siblings. Plait. *Flechten. Zopf. Tranca.* When she was a girl, on the fazenda, Mutter plaited her hair in several ways: in two plaits known as *Zöpfe*; a crown known as a *Haarkranz* or hair-wreath; a *Fischgrätenzopf*, that is, the fishbone plait; a *Bauernzopf*, the Farmer's Plait. The worst of all was the Farmer's Plait, because it pulled her scalp so tightly it made her whole head ache.

The shivering spreads to her teeth. Her jaw trembles, although she doesn't feel cold.

Mrs Roberts regards her with an ominous expression – a mixture of curiosity and sympathy. Seren does not like it. She searches for something pleasant to say about the house. The overlapping rugs, the net curtains, the faintly oriental vases displayed above the fireplace, an immoveable mahogany writing desk like in an Agatha Christie novel.

'My father had a typewriter like that,' she says. It's not a compliment exactly; she'd wanted to pay a compliment. 'It's old, isn't it?'

'Nineteen forty-seven. I'm used to it. I don't like these plastic, tippety contraptions they make now. I'm always mistyping and it takes me longer to correct my mistakes than it does using this old thing.'

'Are you a writer?'

'Oh no. Worse than that. A journalist.'

She laughs at her own joke. Seren smiles back; she wants to ask – what's the difference?

'I write the occasional thing for the Cymmrodorion or Barn when they ask. Doesn't pay very well, but at least it's something to do.' Mrs Roberts picks up her cup, holds it daintily between thumb and forefinger. 'You're rather dark,' she says suddenly.

'I lived in Brazil.'

'So you speak Portuguese?'

'No . . . Not now. Not so much.'

'I'm sure you do. A person can't forget a language. It's always there, somewhere. Lodged in the brain.'

'Yes.'

'A person can't forget, but *people* . . . people often forget their languages. Society is less vigilant, you see. Its memory wavers and changes depending on . . . Well, on whoever's winning the war.'

'What war?'

She takes a cigarette. It's a cigarette like Seren has never seen before: brown like a cigar, but thin as a mechanical pencil.

'Forgive me, but you're not *from* Brazil originally, are you? Your hair is quite light, and your eyes. Your eyes are blue.'

'I grew up in the south. On a farm. It's why I like it here in Wales, I suppose. I like the fields. The freedom. Animals, too.'

'You look like the sort of girl who loves animals.'

Seren tucks her hands between her thighs to keep them still. She puts on her polite voice, the one she's learned from the radio. 'Do you keep any animals, Mrs Roberts?'

'No. I find people's love of animals rather dull.'

'Oh.'

'Llew likes them. He's been insisting I get a dog or a cat for company. He doesn't like the idea of me being alone during the day, but I've told him many times that I am happiest by myself. When you get to a certain age, you don't have much patience for other people's flaws. Your own are enough.'

The coals are catching now. First they burn a bright orange, then the colour grows deeper, becoming vermilion, scarlet, purple. The heat is fierce. Drops of sweat appear on Mrs Roberts' forehead. Seren feels it too, but still she's not *inside* warm. The rain from that morning has trickled into her flesh and pooled in her organs, freezing them. She thinks of Llew. The teacher-hero. He must have been cold, colder than anyone, up there on the mast. For how long was he up there, cold and alone? Now he's sitting in the station. Will they have a change of clothes for him? Will they give him a towel to dry his hair? It was dark, his hair, off-black. But perhaps when dry it was a much lighter shade, because his eyes were grey in the gloom of that morning, but in another light they might be nearer blue than grey . . .

'Are you hungry? Would you like something more substantial?'

'Sorry?'

Mrs Roberts goes to the kitchen, muttering to herself. 'Will the butter be any good this time? I asked him to churn it for me, not get it from the shop, to go up to Evans Brynglas to get the butter from his wife, but he tries to trick me, wrapping up shop-bought butter and pretending he's got it from Evans Brynglas' wife. What's the use of baking your own bread if the butter's no good . . .'

Is she speaking in English or Welsh or another language entirely? One of those mysterious languages she said her husband studied? Languages Seren had never heard of. Breton. Cornish.

Mrs Roberts is back with a tray loaded with earthenware plates, ochre, like the jugs that hung from

the pub walls. On the plates are thick slices of bread
and quivering scoops of pale butter.

'It should be yellow. Yellow,' Mrs Roberts com-
plains, putting the plates on the worn coffee table
by Seren's knee. 'This is whey. In my day, no one
would dare sell this. The most important element of
any meal is the butter. I don't suppose you had much
butter in the south of Brazil.'

Manteiga. The shaking begins again; Seren sits on
her hands.

'I came from a farm. A ranch where we had cows.
Hundreds and hundreds of cows. Vater, I mean, my
father, he looked after them even though he didn't
know anything about cows. My mother made butter,
but she was terrible at it because when she was a
girl it was the servants that made the butter for her
and if she made butter it was only ever for her own
amusement. Mutter hated churning. It took her longer
than anyone else and my father lost his temper. That
was in the beginning before they were able to afford
servants, and Mutter, I mean, Mother, she didn't need
to make any butter after that.'

'You have to have the *knack*,' says Mrs Roberts
slowly. 'That's what your mother was missing, you

see. That special flick of the wrist that turns milk into butter.'

'She missed many things.'

'Where are your parents now?'

Putting her untouched plate of food aside, Seren announces she urgently needs the bathroom. Mrs Roberts tells her to go upstairs, before putting the cigarette, as yet unlit, between her lips.

Seren takes the stairs slowly. They're steep; the banister flimsy and old. Llew's flannel shirt moves against her skin. His trousers are loose around her hips, but not too loose. Why can't all clothes be like men's clothes?

On the landing she has a view into three rooms. The fourth is closed. There's a master bedroom with a bay window from which Mrs Roberts had warned her about the hemlock earlier. It is conservatively furnished: one mirrored wardrobe, a double bed with a red and pink bedspread. Next to it there's a box room with a sewing machine, fabric, old toys. The bathroom is surprisingly large, furnished with a free-standing bath.

She stands in front of the sink for longer than she needs, breathing in magnolia and vanilla. She examines her hands. Yes, they are still trembling. Although not as bad as they were downstairs with Mrs Roberts. The smell makes her think of the pharmacies in the US. The kind that sold large packages of soaps and creams to old ladies. As she stands there, her hands horizontal, she thinks of the brick-sized bar of soap Vater used to wash his skin, hair, clothes, everything. The odourless yellow-white bar that did nothing more than remove the overpowering smell of sweat and animal feed. Rubbing out the day rather than adding anything pleasurable to it. Which is, she thinks, everything you might want to know about that man. He was there. He made life possible for a while. But now that she's making such an effort to remember him, an effort she hasn't made in years, Seren finds that his face is gone, along with his voice and habits . . . She remembers that he existed. And that he was good enough. Like the bar of yellow-white soap.

The shaking is bad now. She sticks her hands under running water. One tap freezes, the other scalds.

Back on the landing, there's a sign hanging on the closed door with the letters L L E. The 'w' has fallen off. She listens but hears nothing. No footsteps. The door handle is antique, made of iron. She holds it and presses her thumb down on the little disc made for thumbs. The latch goes up.

It's obvious, once she steps inside, why the door was closed.

This bedroom is the bedroom of an animal. There's no floor, only clothing. There's no place to lie down, only magazines and books. The drawers hang open. Stacks of identical navy exercise books rise from the ground like fragmented Roman columns. Photographs depict various tall buildings: Tour d'Eiffel, Alexanderturm, Torre pendente di Pisa.

Unlike downstairs, there's nothing pompous or upright about this room; it's like a den, or a sty. That is, it's for the pig alone and not anyone else. No visitors. Apart from other pigs like herself, she thinks.

The bed is interesting: does he sleep on it? Does he sleep under the magazines?

The typewriter is new. One of the 'tippety' contraptions. There's no paper in it.

He's pinned a badge on the lampshade – a green, red and white triangle.

SIONED DAVIES it says on one navy exercise book. YEAR 11. On another ROBAT JOHN. YEAR 10. Do they know their teacher lives like this?

The feathers from his down duvet stick out of the

corners. She touches the bed, because there's no one watching.

She's surprised there are no people in his photographs. She wants to find one of his parents, or a girl. A girlfriend. She wants the room to reveal more than it already has.

Cheap paperback notebooks stick out under his pillow (diaries?). She opens one, filled with pages and pages of ink-smudged handwriting, all in Welsh.

On his windowsill he has propped up a series of postcards: these are different from the others decorating his wardrobe. They're black and white. They're also an odd size, larger than usual, almost rectangular. They show, from left to right: a tram passing imperial buildings; a ship bridge opening in a dockyard; reed-covered sand dunes; a forest glade; a low barn on which a one-legged bird is standing; a line of frail-looking fishing boats.

The bird has two legs, but chooses to stand on one. It's very thin, as if its white body is performing a balancing act on a bamboo shoot. The tips of its wings are black; its beak is tucked in close, half the length of its body. This bird she has seen before. This bird has a name. Oh God, she remembers it now. The name comes from her first language. The language she learned before all other languages. The name before all other names.

Gandras.

The bird takes off into the sky.

Seren collapses on the floor.

GIANT

SHE IS ON a beach, but not a beach she recognises immediately. The waves are not rough and foaming like in Aberystwyth; they're not blue and warm as they are in Porto Alegre. They're grey ripples, pushing onto the flat shoreline. Behind her are undulating dunes and the reeds, feather-headed. The wind blows through the reeds, and they sway lightly.

She knows this place after all. It is the Spit: the strip of land far in the east, between Lithuania and what was once Germany. She remembers it now; feels sure of the place for the first time since she was a child, and as she remembers, words begin spilling into her head – words she knows and yet does not know. She knows that in German, they call this place die Kurische Nehrung. In Lithuanian, Kuršių nerija. She knows that this long line of sand jutting out into the cold, northern sea was made by a giant who knelt at the boundaries of his country and tested how far he could lob his spit across the channel.

As soon as she thinks this, another piece of knowledge arrives in her head: something is coming. It wants to kill her.

No. Best not look. She could swim to safety, but between her and the sea is a thick carpet of *quallen*. Translucent, wobbling balls of dying life, coming from the ocean. She bends down to take a look at the *quallen*. They're so translucent that it's difficult to see how they are able to eat and respire. Inside is beige mucus and black spots. She touches one; the membranes stick to her skin.

People are running along the beach. Away from the terror. Away from the thing that wants to kill her.

People are cycling along the beach too.

Pearl is on a bike. She's naked; she didn't have time to put her clothes on in the rush to escape. She doesn't stop for Seren: she's too afraid. Instead, she shouts – 'Come on! Come with us!'

It's too late. The poison from the see-through jellyfish is working its way through her arms and chest until she can no longer move. Her whole body is paralysed.

Pearl cycles towards the fishing boats in the distance, leaving Seren behind. The waves are picking up, rolling with increased ferocity onto the shore, as if they are frightened too.

The giant. It appears between the dunes. There's something wrong with it. Where there should be a face, there's hair: wild, black hair. It stumbles down onto the beach towards her, arms outstretched, ploughing into the cyclists. He crushes them underfoot like seashells.

He is coming for her.

It is not possible for her to move.

He is as tall as a small hill. He is as naked as a hill. Only, instead of grass, there is abundant hair. She must crane her head to see the furball that is his head. His feet are covered in shards of bicycle and bone. His gait is slow and lumbering. It takes a long time for him to reach her. The feet are as large as cars; the *quallen* are all around her, constructing a fortress of translucent slime. It is not possible to move; she thinks she might vomit and is weeping uncontrollably.

The giant's enormous step arches over her and into the sea. The splash sends a fountain of jelly-stuffed seawater over her head. SPLASH. SPLASH. SPLASH. The sea is choppy now, as the giant runs on into the ocean. Each step creates huge waves. SPLASH. SPLASH. SPLASH.

He does have a face. It is on the back of his head: an ordinary, human face with two eyes, a (hairy) nose and a mouth, hanging open. The giant is looking past her at the land he's leaving behind. The expression is hard to read: injured, perhaps, bewildered, as if his body is acting out of control and he – that is, the face – must simply bear it.

She watches the giant for a long time. His face never goes under the waves: he runs along the bottom of the ocean as his eyes gaze longingly at the shore behind him.

The waves swell, towering in the air, foaming white, before they fly towards her like a mustering of white birds. *Gandras*, she thinks. The storks that nest among the reeds and promise children.

FIREPLACE

THE CUSHION IS wet. Her lips are covered in slime from the *quallen*. No. Not slime. She lifts her head and cries out. It feels as though someone has cracked it open. Not from the jellyfish. From something else. She wipes her mouth with her sleeve. (His sleeve). And discovers that the slime is coming from her nose. Her chin is covered in it.

Kur aš esu? she thinks. No, that's wrong. That makes no sense. She wants to ask: *Wo bin ich?* No, no, wrong again. She is not on the fazenda. She knows she is not with Mutter and Vater. No. If she wants to ask the question she needs to use other words.

Where am I?

There.

The fire is almost out, coals smouldering, giving the last rays of heat. Seren is a child again, curled up on the armchair, and all is silent. The servants are asleep. The farmhands are asleep. The cows and the chickens and the dogs are asleep. And she's alone, abandoned. The tears start coming again – if she weeps someone will come, if she cries out some-one will come downstairs with a lamp and a glass of milk, and they'll stroke her hair and say Marie, *Mariechen ... Mano mergina ...*

No, no.

She's rushing along a road, along the sea, along the reeds, her little legs pumping up and down, up and down; the other children are faster than her, ahead of her, she wants them to wait – wait for me, not so fast, please, wait for me, don't leave me alone again – but the others are laughing and she can see the muscles on the backs of their knees tighten and their long socks falling down as they race to the bay, to the amber-sanded coves and her voice doesn't carry – wait, not so fast, come back, please ...

No, no.

There's a body on the floor. Another corpse. She remembers the pale woman at the window with her white hair and the threadbare sofa where she drank tea in someone else's clothes. She remembers Pearl. She remembers the log cabin at Cae Manon where the three of them slept.

184

Oh, she's here and she feels herself relax, heart slowing. But why is there a body on the floor? It's not the old woman who's lying there. It's a man, still in his coat. His legs are stretched out, an arm tucked under his head.

His eyes are open. 'Hello, Seren.'

She smiles. 'They let you go,' she says.

'For now.'

He touches her forehead with the back of his hand. 'You're hot. You have a temperature.'

There's enough light from the embers to see him and she's glad. He stares up at her, hand under his cheek; he's still wearing his boots, too tired it seems to take them off.

He's whispering to her. She thinks: I will remember every word. This is what he says:

'I thought my prayers had been answered when I saw you by the cliffs. I thought they'd be on me straight away, the police I mean, but no one came. I was there for hours and hours. It was like Christmas Day. Everyone was indoors. And then I saw you. You of all people.' He clears his throat; it makes him sound very old and serious. 'I've seen you in town. I've seen you on the beach with your pals. I always

185

wanted to talk to you. But you were never alone. You were always with others.'

It's the first time she's ever thought of herself that way, as a person who was always *with others*.

'Until yesterday morning. You were alone yesterday.'

She bites her lip, remembering the lonely walk to the field; the pleasant vertigo of looking up at the kite and then down at the waves; of coming close. She was not afraid of heights. She was not afraid of the sea either.

'What were you doing out there?'

'Walking.'

'You were walking very near to the edge. Did you know that?'

'The world must look different from the top of a TV mast.'

'You can see the world much better from up there.'

She tells him: 'It was the first time I'd ever ridden a bike. My first time.'

He laughs like he doesn't believe her, but she perseveres: 'I was planning to just push your bike to the telephone box. I didn't think I'd be able to do it properly and then . . . and then it just happened. Like my body knew what to do. Can you understand that?'

'You must have learned when you were a child.'

'When I was a child we only had one bike and I wasn't allowed on it, because I might hurt myself. It was forbidden. So, you see, I never learned.'

'Did you like it?'

'Yes.'

'I'm glad. Something good has come out of it all then. Your rediscovery of the humble bicycle.'

'Discovery not rediscovery,' she says, a little too harshly. 'I told you it was the first time I'd been on one.'

Llew turns again so he's lying on his back, staring at the ceiling. 'I admire your courage,' he says.

'What courage? I wasn't the one up the mast.'

'You never answered Cai's questions.'

'Who?'

'The police officer. The young one.'

'With the spots?'

'He was livid. He kept trying to persuade Jones they should bring you in. It would have been easy to play along, but you didn't.'

'That wasn't bravery,' she says. 'Anyway, I did answer his questions. I told him my name, Seren Gold, and my age, which is twenty-nine.'

'It's not your real name,' he says quietly.

'I don't know what you mean. What makes a *real* name, anyway? It's as real as any other. If I hear someone calling Seren, I turn my head. That's enough.'

'What name were you born with?'

There's a clock ticking in the room; a loud, steady beat. She wonders why she hasn't heard it before. Now she can't hear anything else.

She kicks the blanket off and eases herself from the sofa onto the floor. He shifts to make room for her and she presses herself against him. The new development renders him silent. She's trying to do what she has always done: break down a wall without having to reveal too much. Her mouth is by his mouth, their toes touch. She has to balance her arm along her side so as not to hug him too soon. Her eyes are still wet.

'Did I cry in my sleep?'

'Yes,' he says. 'And you talked. I couldn't follow most of what you said. I think, at one point, you were speaking German. I understood you then.'

'What did I say?'

'*Not so fast.*'

'That's all?'

'You asked for your mother. You said Mutti.'

'I don't have a mother.'

'Oh,' he says, and there is another silence, in which she can hear him deciding what to do. Ask her more questions, or leave it be? He clears his throat and begins to stroke her hair. He's nervous, the hero-teacher. She can tell by the way his breath quickens and how he so carefully avoids touching her skin. She closes her eyes, whispers in the dark:

'I was adopted and taken to Brazil when I was four.'

'Where were you born?'

'My German passport says Tilsit. My Brazilian passport says Sovetsk. I don't call it anything.'

He touches her skin. His thumb trailing down her cheek and lips.

'It's a border town. It was Lithuanian and German and now it's Russian. I was young when they found me, only four years old they said, but no one can say for sure. It was the last year of the war and everything was destroyed. There was an army of lost children like me. I wasn't the only one. I didn't know my surname. I didn't know the name of my parents, whoever they were. Mutter said I was found sitting on a pile of clothes in the snow.'

'Do you want to go back there?'

'No, I don't.' There, the harsh voice again. Horrible, when everything is so soft and intimate. Where

189

does it come from?' 'Sometimes I remember words from back then. Not German exactly ... I think they're Lithuanian. They come out of nowhere. When I'm tired or ... I've taken something, I'll have this ... urge to speak a language I've forgotten.'

'You haven't forgotten it.'

'Oh yes I have. I have. It's gone. Only sometimes it comes back.'

'Isn't that wonderful?'

'No. It's frightening. A horror film. Words that aren't mine popping into my head. Words I don't understand myself. There's a part of me that isn't – *mine.*'

A pause. The strokes are long, from the top of her head to the ends of her hair. A thumb brushes her cheek.

'I'm not explaining it well. I sound mad.'

'No.'

'It's like having a dark room inside you. Locked. You never go in. But from time to time you hear voices coming from the other side ...'

He's caressing her neck now. Her arm is on his back, holding him close. The fire is out but they are warm.

'I've never heard a voice like yours before,' he says.

'And I've never heard a name like yours.'

'It means lion.'

'Mine means star. I found it in an astrology text-book in the New York Public Library.'

'It's a good name for you.'

'Ble mae'r Gymraeg?' she recites her Welsh from his banner. 'What does it mean?'

'*Where's the Welsh?*'

'I have some. Dai Trisant taught me a little. Listen. *Defaid. Ci. Cath. Barcud. Buwch. Adar. Lygoden.*'

'Very good. But it's *ll*ygoden for mouse. Like *ll*ew for lion. You have to stick your tongue behind your teeth. The tip of your tongue. That's it. And then blow. Blow out *sharply*.'

She does as he asks, breathes out. It sounds more like a screech than his faint, low hiss.

'Almost. You have to curl it a little.' He puts his forefinger in her mouth, presses the top of her tongue. 'Now touch your teeth. There. That's the right shape.'

His finger tastes of salt.

'*Ll*ygoden,' she says. '*Ll*ew,' she says and kisses him.

FEVER

THE CLOCK RETURNS, chiming its maddening silver chime. When she opens her eyes, she's back on the sofa again and it's daytime.

She thinks she's cured (Llew has cured her), but this isn't the case. When she raises her arm, she finds it doesn't go very far. There's a strange weakness in her limbs, and her body seems both very light (she hasn't eaten, can't eat) and very heavy.

Someone has left a plate of toast on the stained coffee table. There's a black boot underneath the table and, attached to the boot, a leg. She cranes her head. To the leg, she adds a trouser suit, a wide jacket, a pearl necklace. The woman is speaking to her: she's a doctor. Seren has a fever. A chest infection. She will have to take antibiotics three times a day. Is she listening?

Seren nods.

The strange woman says she's lucky Mrs Roberts is letting her stay. It would be worse to go back to those log cabins in the woods. How does she know where Seren lives? In any case, if Seren had the strength, she would explain how good it is at Cae Manon. They're more than capable of making long-lasting fires, just like Mrs Roberts. You don't need a house for keeping warm. Jim is in charge of the hearth. Pearl knits and sews. The blankets are from Scotland: down-stuffed quilts, patchwork quilts. Anything you like. They have sheep-wool rugs, too. Has the doctor ever slept under sheep's wool? It keeps the coldest winters at bay. And at Cae Manon, she'd be surrounded by the people she loved.

'Why are you crying?' asks the doctor. 'Are you in any pain?'

She shakes her head. Mrs Roberts walks around to face her. She is all in black, the same outfit as the day before, hands on her hips, ready to fix something. She turns to the doctor and they speak in Welsh.

Llew perches by her feet, mug in hand, looking anxious. He leans over and translates what the two women are saying: all the things she can do to get better. Drink beef tea. Stay warm. Avoid exertion.

'Why don't you eat something? Or here, drink

this.' Llew kneels by the side of the sofa, offers the mug to her like a pilgrim, but she turns away.

The woman doctor in her nice trouser suit leaves her medicine in a brown glass bottle.

'*Diolch*,' says Mrs Roberts. This means 'thank you'.

Dai Trisant is on the doorstep. He won't come in because he has to get off. The two collies circle his legs. Mrs Roberts and Llew stand either side. They look worried.

Seren observes them from the sofa. This has been made easier by a cushion Llew placed behind her during breakfast. She sits up, hands folded where the blanket pools between her legs, following the Welsh talk as best she can. Mrs Roberts' hair is in a Fishbone Plait. Painfully neat. Earlier she had her hands on her hips, now they are folded. She seems to be becoming more and more unhappy.

Llew says to Dai Trisant, 'You'll have to come in and explain to her.'

English sounds very strange all of a sudden, surprising the conversation like that. They switch back to Welsh.

Mrs Roberts waves her arms: No it's best if she's left to sleep, she seems to say.

Dai looks over his shoulder: Why am I here and not at the farm? he seems to ask.

Llew spreads his arms. 'Come on. We need to tell her.'

'Tell me what?'

Three faces turn to her at once. Llew is smiling, but Mrs Roberts looks aggrieved and Dai looks more tired than anything. The collies want to greet her, but Dai tells them to Sit Down. Be Quiet.

'Make sure you keep them there,' says Mrs Roberts, arms tightening around her waist.

And so Dai addresses Seren from the doorway. 'They tell me you've got a fever.'

She nods.

'Bad luck.'

'Why are you in town?'

'I was coming to that.' He points at a potato sack that's been dumped on the porch. The sack reads: SIR BENFRO. TATWS. 'I went out this morning and found this by the gate.'

'What, potatoes?'

'No . . .' He bends over and takes out a tanned bundle of suede and fur. Her heart beats faster. 'This coat is yours, isn't it? I've seen you wear it.'

'I don't want it.'

'But it is yours?'

'It belongs to them.'

'You mean your friends at Cae Manon?'

'Yes. Give it back.'

Dai folds the coat carefully and lays it on top of the sack. His gaze moves between Llew and the floor. Llew nods encouragement.

'I can't.'

'Why not?'

'They left this morning. There's no one there.'

She says, 'No.'

'I'm afraid so, *bach*. Pritchards gave them a lift to Holyhead. He's got that big Morris Minor and he managed to get a good chunk of their things in the back. He was telling me the one girl had a rabbit in her pocket.'

She makes a sound that isn't quite laughter. 'What are you talking about?'

Dai shrugs. 'Well. There you are.'

'Where were they going?' asks Llew.

'Ireland,' Dai replies.

'Why?'

'Heaven only knows.'

Bastard. Ancestral! He can go fuck himself. At the same time, she thinks: No. There has been a mistake.

They could not have gone without her, without saying goodbye, without patching things up. It isn't possible. Dai Trisant doesn't understand that they belong together: Jim, Pearl and Seren. No one understands.

'This,' says Mrs Roberts, nudging the sack with her foot. 'Is this really all your belongings?'

But there's the sack to prove it. She can't ignore it, even if she tries. Jim did this. Jim and his obsession with Ireland, his obsession with himself. Fucking traitor lying fucking bastard. And Pearl – she can't bear to think about Pearl, folding her things, stuffing them into a potato sack.

'I don't want it.' It comes out as a shout. Mrs Roberts turns to her grandson, but Llew is not looking at anyone but her.

She shouldn't have a sack at all. The blankets didn't belong to anyone, neither did the quilts, or the coats and mittens. They shared everything; made everything together. That's why she doesn't want the coat. It's true she had it with her when Pearl picked her up at the station in Maine five years ago. But once she'd decided to stay with them, travel the world with them, the coat was as much Pearl's as hers. Jim's too if he'd wanted it.

Fucking sleazy hypocritical preachy fucking bastard.

Llew brings the sack in and as he does so the dogs follow. Dai orders them to stay, but it's too late. One of them is already nuzzling her neck. The other is sniffing around the typewriter.

She thinks, There is nothing more beautiful on earth than these animals. Humans can all go fuck themselves.

But some people disagree.

Mrs Roberts is shouting, 'Not in my front room! Not in my house!' She shoos them off, almost stepping on their paws as she does so. One runs back to his master. The other slinks off before returning, ignoring Mrs Roberts' protestations. He presses his wet nose against Seren's shoulder.

She whispers, '*Ci*. I love you.'

Mrs Roberts tries to grab it, but Llew puts his hand on her arm.

'Mam, stop it now. It's only a dog.'

'You know your father's allergic to the fur.'

'He's not here now, is he?'

'Oh, get out of my way.'

The dog scampers between Llew's legs, who stumbles, sending the breakfast table flying. Tea splatters over the rug, the china cup is in pieces. Mrs Roberts claps her hands to her mouth and groans.

'*Duw, duw*. What is all this?'

It's the policemen: Sergeant Jones and the boy, Cai. They take it in turns to give Dai Trisant a forceful slap on the back, before stepping inside.

'The dog...' Dai begins, but Cai has already got the collie by the scruff of the neck. He drags it out of the room, throwing it at Dai's feet. But the collie doesn't give up. As soon as Cai lets go, it tries to scamper back to Seren. This time, when Cai grabs its neck, he hits the collie sharply on the nose. Twice, three times, until the dog whines and hides behind his master with his tail between his legs.

'That was uncalled for,' says Mrs Roberts coolly.

Cai smiles. Dai Trisant, on the other hand, says nothing. He simply turns and leaves. His dogs at his heel.

'Wait!' Seren calls, getting up from the sofa. 'Please!' She wants to know if he was lying. If they're really gone. If Cae Manon is just a field with an empty shed and a cold hearth. But a wave of dizziness hits her and she's forced to stop. She holds her head in her hands while the world rights itself.

'What the hell are you wearing?' says the Boy

Policeman, laughing at her check shirt and cord trousers. His acne is redder than usual. In fact, he seems to be bleeding from the chin. 'Isn't this the woman you said you didn't know, Llew?' he goes on.

'I didn't know her until yesterday.'

'Didn't know her until yesterday but now she's wearing your clothes and sleeping on your sofa?'

'My sofa,' says Mrs Roberts. 'She came to return Llew's bike. Then she fell ill and she's been here since. Nothing more to it.'

Cai doesn't look at Mrs Roberts; he pretends they are alone. He is standing a little too close: he smells unnatural, like the fake pine smell people put in their cars. 'Your friends have skipped town. On their way to Holyhead apparently. A little suspicious, don't you think?'

'What?'

'No. I suppose you have no idea. Just as you have no idea where you are or who he is or what your name is or anything else.'

'You shouldn't scratch your spots. Every child knows that,' she says.

'Do you want to spend the night in a cell?'

'Now, now,' says the sergeant. 'Llew. We've got a few questions for you down at the station.'

'I've already told you everything.'

'Well,' says Sergeant Jones. 'You know how it is.'

Mrs Roberts strides forward, imperious. She delivers a long speech in Welsh. The men listen politely, but it seems to have little effect. At the end, the sergeant points at the door and says, 'After you.'

'No,' Seren says. 'You're not taking him now. He can't go now.'

'I'm afraid we can't rearrange at a more suitable time, Miss Gold.'

'No,' she says, and finds herself blocking the doorway.

'Now, now,' says the sergeant again. He looks unhappy, and Llew looks unhappy, but the Boy Policeman grins at her.

'You can't take him. He has to stay. If you take him away I'll kill myself.'

'Now, no need for that.'

'Crazy bitch,' Cai mutters.

She pushes him without thinking, just a little push. His chest is scrawny and hard; all chest bone and ribs. He staggers back, more out of surprise than force, before slapping her across the face. Mrs Roberts screams. Llew charges forward but the sergeant comes between them.

'That's enough. Enough.' He grabs Llew and steers him out of the front door with one hand while pulling Cai after him with the other. Llew stops, turns as if to go back but the sergeant gives him a sharp shove. It is the sergeant who looks back, says goodbye to the women: 'I'm sorry about this, Mrs Roberts. Miss Gold.'

She can't feel the slap. Is it possible? It has made her warm. It has cured her dizziness.

'My child, are you all right?' Mrs Roberts steers her to the sofa. 'Shhh. Have a sit-down. There. Shhhh.'

Seren can see the old woman's scalp where the plait is pulling at her skin. Don't pull so hard. Don't pull me, Mutter. Don't. It hurts. Oh it hurts. I don't want it.

'Leave me alone!'

She runs after them, taking the coat with her as she goes. She tries to sprint to the gates, but she's so weak. She stumbles and she collapses next to the black pond. The path blurs and sways in front of her eyes, as though she's fainted in the desert heat. The police car is already halfway down the road. She calls his name, but she doesn't know if she's calling it right, making the right sound with her tongue because he's gone.

First Jim, then Pearl, now Llew.

She's alone. So alone. Fucking bastard. Fucking police. Fucking human beings.

'Seren!' Mrs Roberts calls after her, but she can't face being the convalescent now.

She pulls the coat on, picks herself up; keeps going. Loping past the nice driveways and the statues of lions and the Grecian columns and the bungalows. On to the main road. Crossing the stone bridge. Her cheek is smarting with anger. Fucking bastard. Lying. Hypocritical. Cockroaches.

The police car has vanished. But she keeps going until she reaches the marina, with the Welsh flags rattling the boats. Keeps on until she reaches the sea wall, where the waves are high and rough, and where there are stairs that lead down to nowhere. Stairs that are swallowed up by the tide.

The seagulls are being blown here and there, like messages from across the sea. They fight on, but the wind keeps them where it wants, like a hand, pinning them.

Out on a craggy spit, there's a woman picking living things from rock pools. The wind whips her scarf up and away.

Seren puts her hands in her coat pocket. But her pockets fight back.

She takes out a pair of grey knitting needles. They belong to Pearl, she recognises them. They are the same needles she used to make Seren's clothes, the leg warmers, the cardigan that's hanging from her shoulders, stretched with rainwater. Taped around the ends is a slip of paper with words in Pearl's hand-writing: *So you can make your own.*

But I don't want to.

So you can make your own.

I can't do it.

So you can make your own.

I don't know how.

So you can make your own.

Not without you.

The woman out on the rocks is moving slowly. She's bent double: it's impossible to see how old she is. Only that she's alone, and that the sea is slowly rising to meet her. On the far side of the sea, there's a shadow on the horizon, like a giant lying on its side. Another country, rising out of the dusk.

So that's Ireland, she thinks. I've seen it now.

Seren presses the grey needles to her chest and watches the solitary figure below, a bag slung over her shoulder for cockles, perhaps, or laver. The figure scours the rocks, moving ever closer to the waves.

Seren closes her eyes. The sea blows its salt air on her skin; she can taste it on her lips. She opens her eyes again, casts one last look at that other country, the shadow-line in the distance, before turning away and heading for the police station.

HOMETOWN TALES

Original Tales by Regional Writers

HOMETOWN TALES
BIRMINGHAM

**MARIA WHATTON
STEWART LEE**

Original Tales by Regional Writers

HOMETOWN TALES
GLASGOW

**KIRSTY LOGAN
PAUL MCQUADE**

Original Tales by Regional Writers

HOMETOWN TALES
HIGHLANDS & HEBRIDES

**COLIN MACINTYRE
ELLEN MACASKILL**

Original Tales by Regional Writers

HOMETOWN TALES
LANCASHIRE

**JENN ASHWORTH
BENJAMIN WEBSTER**

AVAILABLE NOW FROM W&N

Original Tales by Regional Writers

HOMETOWN TALES
MIDLANDS

KERRY YOUNG
CAROLYN SANDERSON

Original Tales by Regional Writers

HOMETOWN TALES
SOUTH COAST

GEMMA CAIRNEY
JUDY UPTON

Original Tales by Regional Writers

HOMETOWN TALES
WALES

TYLER KEEVIL
ELUNED GRAMICH

Original Tales by Regional Writers

HOMETOWN TALES
YORKSHIRE

CATHY RENTZENBRINK
VICTORIA HENNISON

AVAILABLE NOW FROM W&N